Praise for *Rearming Hinduism*

"The best study available on th[is topic in the] media age."

"A delightful, delightful book."

"I recommend it highly."

       -Arvind Sharma, Birks Professor of Comparative Religion, McGill University

"Very readable. Well argued."
       - Dr. Subramaniam Swamy

"A valiant attempt at opening up a third space."
       - *India Currents*

"Demands and deserves attention."
       - *The Hindu*

"A must read for those who wish to experience what it means to be Hindu."
       - *The Pioneer*

"A milestone."
       - *India Facts*

"For all who care about Hinduism, humanity and the planet."
       - Jeffery Long, Professor of Religion, Elizabethtown College and Swami Vivekananda Chair, Belur Math

"In a very personal and intimate voice, Juluri ties together his ideas eruditely using theoretical models that identify and deconstruct Hinduphobia in academia."
       - Yvette Rosser, author, *Curriculum as Destiny*

"Among the bold voices heralding our 21st century Hindu renaissance. Impossibly traditional and 21st century."
       - Paramacharya Sadasivanathaswami, *Hinduism Today*

REARMING HINDUISM

Vamsee Juluri is a professor of media studies at the University of San Francisco. He is the author of *The Mythologist: A Novel* (Penguin India), *Bollywood Nation: India through its Cinema* (Penguin India), *The Hanuman Trilogy* (Westland, forthcoming) and *The Guru Within* (Westland, forthcoming).

VAMSEE JULURI

REARMING HINDUISM

NATURE, HINDUPHOBIA, AND THE RETURN OF INDIAN INTELLIGENCE

westland ltd
61, II Floor, Silverline Building, Alapakkam Main Road,
Maduravoyal, Chennai 600 095
93, I Floor, Sham Lal Road, Daryaganj, New Delhi 110 002

First published by westland ltd 2015

Copyright © Vamsee Juluri 2015

Cover photo: Chetan Sandhir

Calligraphy: Poosapati Parameshwar Raju

Photographs:
Mark Ulyseas (Pages 54, 72, 115, 126, 144, 160, 174)
Lakshmi Prabhala (Pages 25, 26, 40, 116)
Sadhana Ramchander (Pages vi, 94, 188)

Design and typesetting: BluePencil Infodesign, Hyderabad, India

10 9 8 7 6

ISBN: 978-93-84030-52-0

Printed at Thomson Press (India) Ltd.

Disclaimer

Due care and diligence has been taken while editing and printing the book, neither the Author, Publisher nor the Printer of the book hold any responsibility for any mistake that may have crept in inadvertently. Westland Ltd, the Publisher and the printers will be free from any liability for damages and losses of any nature arising from or related to the content. All disputes are subject to the jurisdiction of competent courts in Chennai.

This book is sold subject to the condition that it shall not by way of trade or otherwise, be lent, resold, hired out, circulated, and no reproduction in any form, in whole or in part (except for brief quotations in critical articles or reviews) may be made without written permission of the publishers.

www.rearminghinduism.com

For my father, Professor J V Ramana Rao.
A life lived in the *sanathana* of this *dharma*.
A life lived in the Greatest Love.
And from him, to you, in these words.

November 16, 1928–November 10, 2014

अग्निर्मे वाचि श्रितः ।
वाग्घृदये । हृदयं मयि ।
अहममृते अमृतं ब्रह्मणि ॥

ईशानो मे मन्यौ श्रितः ।
मन्युर्हृदये । हृदयं मयि ।
अहममृते अमृतं ब्रह्मणि ॥

Agni expresses himself in my words.
Let my words be inspired from my heart.
Let me always be established in the Divine who is immortal.

Ishana (Rudra) expresses himself in me as righteous anger.
May the righteous anger in me be guided by the Divine in my heart.
Let me always be established in the Divine who is immortal.

(From: Sri Rudraprashnah Laghunyaasah, Veda Pushpanjali, Volume 2
Compiled by M. Sai Roopak)

CONTENTS

Preface: Your Hinduism	1
Part 1. *Desa Kala Dosha:* The Ideologies of Hinduphobia	25
1. The Academic Maya Sabha	27
2. The Myth of an 'Alternative History'	41
3. The Myth of Aryan Origins	55
4. The Myth of Vedic Violence	73
5. The Myth of a Hindu History Without a Hindu View of God	95
Part 2. *Sanathana:* A Hindu View of God	115
1. Civilization: A Prelude	117
2. Tvameva, You Alone (Vedopanishad)	127
3. Cousins and Friends (Krishna and Rama)	145
4. The Greatest Love (Dasavatar)	161
5. Teacher (The Gita)	175
Conclusion: *Jagat Guru*	189
Notes	203
Acknowledgements	230

For a civilization is not just buildings and machines, but its people, their thought, and their culture. It is a way of knowing the world, a way of giving meaning and value to the contents of life.

Preface

YOUR HINDUISM

You are an achievement.

You may not fully know *why* just yet. But you have probably felt, in some quiet way, the fact that you belong to something significant that has come before you in history. You might not always know how to express that feeling, but you know that it inspires you, and elevates you.

You belong to the one civilization that still stands much as it once did even after all these thousands of years of human history; thousands of years of wars, conquest, pillage, subjugation, desecration and devastation, thousands of years of supposed progress that have given us a world today that runs on brutal violence against nature, life and the planet itself.

You belong to a civilization that is still standing, but surrounded as it were, by a mess, in India and across the whole world, of environmental devastation, cultural confusion, ethical indifference, and economic insecurity.

But still, it stands. Still, there is hope.

For a civilization is not just buildings and machines, but its people, their thought, and their culture. It is a way of knowing the world, a way of giving meaning and value to the contents of life.

It is a resource, most of all, for living intelligently. It is a form of culture, an expression of sensibility, a way of harmonizing science, philosophy, and ethics in a people's every thought, word and deed. You can call it a religion, a way of life, or a civilization, you can call it what you will. But no word will suffice.

A billion people on this earth still call God by the same names that people did thousands of years ago. What exists on this earth unchanged for that long? What religion exists on this earth for that long, when so many people have distorted religion and dragged it down from being about love and freedom to being about hatred, coercion and war?

Hinduism could have been wiped out a long time ago.

***

But it wasn't.

You are here.

You still adore and worship your *Ganesha*, your *Hanuman*, your *Shiva*, *Vishnu*, *Lakshmi* and *Parvathi*, and *Rama* and *Krishna* and *Subramanya*. You still have your name as did your forefathers. And you are able to deal as a friend and equal today with people of many faiths and races. It is an accomplishment unlike any other.

It is not a boast but a fact.

Your culture's existence is a triumph of survival.

Your existence is a triumph of survival.

 We belong to a moment in history when Hinduism is beginning to wake up, if not from a long slumber, then at least a long silence.

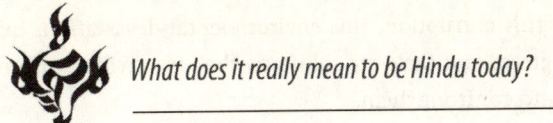 *What does it really mean to be Hindu today?*

In you, in your life, is something that should be studied, preserved, and revered like a work of art in a museum. It may be all messy or mixed up, with good and not so good *sensibilities*; like how you can see *Krishna* in an exquisite ancient sculpture and also in a crude animation form. Hindu civilization is like that, all mixed up. But still, its greatest and most sublime elements are still here, and they are in you. These must not be worn lightly.

You must remember.

We came from a world of wisdom we can barely fathom in today's terms.

And we are here, still.

***

We belong to a moment in history when Hinduism is beginning to wake up, if not from a long slumber, then at least a long silence. We did not speak to the world, and to ourselves, *as Hindus*, in a very long time. For reasons of strategy, and sensibility, we have been modest and easy-going about religion, despite some unpleasant encounters in history with forces to the contrary. For nearly three generations before us, from the time of India's nominal independence in 1947 to the present moment of exuberant hope in 2014, Hinduism has been a religion lived in silence. We prayed, no doubt, and we went to temples and we made deals with God. We enjoyed our festivals and sang our *bhajans* and watched our *Ramayan* serials. But we did not ask, until the present generation came of age really, that provocative question: *what does it really mean to be Hindu today?*

We did not really stop and say, these are the problems in the world today; this corruption, this environmental devastation, this cruelty, this greed, and *these* are solutions that our civilization can teach us now to confront them.

We remained passive. We took Hinduism to be no more than our faith in God, and our ceremonies and customs. But now, we ask, who are we?

How did we make it this far?

What does the future hold for us?

***

This book advances an unusual claim, neither entirely academic, nor entirely spiritual, though it engages critically with the dismal academic approach to Hinduism in the first part, and gazes adoringly at the feet of the spiritual promise of Hinduism, in the second. Underlying both parts though is an insight you might have felt, but perhaps not quite always articulated (and it is not your fault if you did not have the words for it; for sixty years our government neglected the cultivation of its people's own finest qualities in the educational system, tapping and selling our engineering genius but not much else).

The key premise is simply this:

Hinduism is about intelligence, more than anything else.

After all, we have survived and come this far not because of some brutish physical might, or capacity for cruel and annihilating destruction, but because our civilization's reverence for intelligence has underscored its attitudes to nature, culture, human agency, force, restraint, and, some might say, its destiny itself.

And this was not intelligence of the sort demanded for survival in a brutal TV reality-show competition on an island, but a more elegant and life-adoring form of intelligence. It helped us balance our yearning and sense of surrender to the divine with our determination to remain strong and purposeful as humans. It helped us recognize where our agency, our free will, was necessary, and where we had to surrender our egotism to greater forces that guide our hands. It was, and is, still, not an intelligence demeaned to the service of lesser goals like selfish individual advancement, exploitation of others, unequal profit, cruelty and relentless destruction (though some of this has been done in the past because of forces then beyond our control).

It was the intelligence, simply, of a civilization that began its days in prayer before the rising sun asking the divine not for a good kill in a hunt, not for death to enemies, not even for some mythical paradise in afterlife, but only for — intelligence.

It was the mark of a civilization whose most ancient sacred chant says:

May your life-giving rays awaken my intelligence.

May your life-giving rays awaken my intelligence so that I may see You.

And in that exultant joy of worthy sacred adoration that is You,

Know this, that there is only You.

We pray not for unverifiable pleasures in the afterlife. Not for material gain in this, but just for the wisdom to know happiness, light, and joy; for the wisdom to know truth.

The Gayatri Mantra, again, rendered even more simply[1]:

O Light

Let me see that

You are Light.

***

 Hinduism to me is more than a religion, and even more than a way of life. To me, Hinduism is essentially *a way of knowing life*, intelligently.

Long before we reduced prayer to deals with god for goodies and stuff, we were praying for one thing only, and that was simply *the intelligence to see things as they are*.

Millennia later, Mahatma Gandhi was leading us to sing and ask Ishwar-Allah for the same thing too, *sanmathi*, equal-mindedness.

Six decades after the *seeming* collapse of the great promise of the Mahatma, we are back in the realm of intelligence once again, at Mother *Saraswathi's* feet. We called it strength, governance, dynamism, but beyond these inadequate words, we know what really won the day in 2014. It was intelligence, and more importantly, the *recognition*, in our public discourses, of intelligence as the most vital part of our civilizational heritage, and our future. No matter what the critics may think, the present moment in India is not about pride and posturing, of trying to prove our past is greater than someone else's past, much less about trying to prove our religion is better than someone else's religion. It is simply about returning to the core of our civilizational self-understanding, which is to respect intelligence, and let it guide our actions and affairs.

The *Sanathana Dharma*. We might call it Nature's Intelligence. It is a way that sees the wisdom in preserving life, and minimizing pain.

It works, even in the face of great odds, in the face of great forces of destructiveness and ignorance.

All the ancient civilizations we read about in our history books are nothing but names now, devoid of the power of their descendants to even know their past accurately, forced to accept sterile conqueror's fantasies as truth about their past.

As for that 'modern civilization', one might say, like Mahatma Gandhi, that it would be a good idea! While we acknowledge that it is based in intelligence too, we have to point out that it is the sort of intelligence that makes us smart enough to fly to the moon but also oblivious to the destructiveness of a very costly way of life. It is like enjoying the warmth from a raging wildfire as it devours the whole planet. Today's science and technology is not nature's intelligence. It is artificial intelligence, unnatural intelligence. We can do that one too successfully, just as we can speak English, wear suits and ties, just do what it takes. But we must recognize that all of this worldview we take for granted today, all that we learn and accept as truth in the modern world, is rooted in an artificial, technocratic epistemology (a phrase we will discuss later in the book, suffice it to translate from academese for now as: machine-like thinking). You probably know what this epistemology has done to its depiction of Hinduism's wisdom (if you don't, you will see in the first half of this book). You can imagine what else it must be getting wrong about the big questions of life.

We will examine this worldview closely in the first part of this book. As a professor of media studies, that is what I teach and write about, how the worldviews, assumptions, commonsense ideas about our selves and the world, might actually be distortions, myths, and outright lies. My field has challenged many such assumptions in recent years, particularly about gender, race, caste and class. It has however, drawn a complete blank when it comes to Hindus, Hinduism and India. With this book, I try to make amends, and to provide the intellectual groundwork for media students, academics, and just intelligent human beings who care about the world and its lives, to expand their horizons and imagination. My aim is not to praise one group of people and condemn another. It is only to show us how recognizing Hinduism's vitality is going to require a much more radical dismantling of today's commonsense worldview than we have imagined so far. I believe that it is far more than the stray personal prejudices of people of other cultures that have distorted Hinduism. Hinduism to me is more than a religion, and even more than a way of life. To me, Hinduism is essentially *a way of knowing life*, intelligently. When Hinduism is distorted, by either ignorance from outside or complacence from within, a very smart way of knowing the world—perhaps we could even call it nature's way of knowing the world—is distorted. Conversely, a world in which nature is demeaned and destroyed cannot understand Hinduism accurately either, and resorts to low and mean tactics against it.

***

Hinduism has travelled very far down the depths of time. Its future is now wide before us too, and it is a promising one.

That future is in each and every child who lives on this earth today, and wonders: what exactly is this world of gods and goddesses that my parents so revere? It is in every student and seeker, every teenager and every parent, who wonders: why is it that I feel, still, something in the presence of these gods and goddesses that no one else is able to explain?

That sense of wonder is important. Our comic book imagery and cartoon-DVD mythologies and history textbooks that do little more than regurgitate names and dates (and increasingly bloodshed and beheadings) should not replace the spirit of intellectual inquiry about our own thought.

It is only from a sense of wonder that the questions a civilization that cherishes intelligence needs to ask now it will come.

What is God? Who are our Gods? Why is it that nobody has been able to explain what all of this means? Were these Gods great

 Rebuilding Hindu civilization is something that every one of us must be doing, one personal, meaningful vision of Hinduism at a time.

human beings who lived long ago? Were they symbols of natural phenomena? Were they mere superstitions? If so, why do they still feel endearing to us? Why do our art, sculpture, culture, science, philosophy, poetry, music, revolve so much around them? Why do we feel their kindness, protection and wisdom so palpably?

We must listen to these questions, for we probably contemplated them too, when we were younger. We probably made our own conclusions, but for the most part, we went on praying, going to temples, fulfilling vows, without debating what it meant very much.

And then, there are the other questions too, questions not about our philosophy or our Gods, but about these strange times we live in, and the strange insults and lies they heap on our sacred sensibilities and values, the questions that our children who are growing up abroad ask with ever greater urgency.

Why do movies depict us as turbanned snake-charmers, beggars, or snake-eaters?

Why do some people say our tradition is to blame for India's poverty, or our religion for the caste-system? Or for violence against women?

Why is it that our history books do not tell us the truth of who we are and what we are?

Why does this modern world seem so unable to recognize our inner world of tradition? Why do we not speak to the modern world as Hindus? Not as fundamentalists, not as apologists, but simply as intelligent observers who have been on this earth long enough to know a few things about it?

We have seen much of history. We have come from an intellectual tradition concerned with nature and life rather than dogma and ritual. We have come from a worldview in which the cruelty, destructiveness, and sheer unsustainability of today's world should be obvious. Yet, we do not speak, for we do not remember.

We have adjusted much, over the centuries, not just with other people, but with other ideas too. It was inevitable, perhaps, and not always unwelcome. But a time comes when we need to ask if we have adjusted too much, if we have become parrots instead, repeating the clichés and ideologies of the time instead of clearing the morass of ignorance with one magnificent lion's roar.

***

If you are a parent of a Hindu child, there is one more question you need to ask yourself too: if you, or your children, do not find intelligent answers for these questions, will your Hinduism still remain when they grow up, or when their children come?

Maybe you believe that Hinduism is just fine, and the ignorance of those who do not understand it will not affect us. After all, have we not survived so long? Have we not been smart? Did we not invent flying-chariots and missiles thousands of years ago as our *Ramayana* and *Mahabharatha* comics and movies seem to suggest? And are we not doing quite well now? We are successful. We have scientists and CEOs everywhere. We are considered a model minority in foreign countries. We build our temples. We enjoy our Yoga and our wisdom being discovered by everyone. We are annoyed though by some of our politicians and intellectuals who deny us our hard-earned rights, but otherwise, all is well. We might even be feeling triumphant that someone who respects Hindu sentiments has won the election.

But what we don't quite realize is this. May 2014 is only a beginning, a kick back upward from history's rock-bottom. There will be, and there already, is an intellectual and political backlash. Another concern is that triumphalism can easily become complacency, and even arrogance. It has happened before. It cannot happen now. Rebuilding India is the mandate that India might have given its new leader. But rebuilding Hindu civilization is something that every one of us must be doing, one personal, meaningful vision of Hinduism at a time. It has to be done, because even our Gods and Goddesses, even our past glories, real and imagined, and most of all, even our success and pride, cannot guarantee the survival of Hinduism if we do not intellectually confront the existential challenge threatening Hinduism today.

***

Consider this:

A prestigious university in America, a few years ago; the name of a cultural organization for students from the Indian subcontinent suddenly comes under fire. Its name, some believe, is discriminatory, communalist and hateful...

Discrimination has no place in a decent world. Racist names deserve to be called out, condemned, changed—that is the only way oppressed communities can resist oppression; African-Americans, Native Americans, women, oppressed caste communities in India, all have challenged the demeaning names they were once given by groups that had power over them. If the name of the cultural organization was like that, it deserved to be condemned.

If.

If the name was something else, and not *'Sanskriti'*[2].

'Sanskriti'. A word that means culture. A word that means, not just culture in the sterile sense of books and paintings, but culture in the Indian sense of ethics, aesthetics, conduct, civilization itself;

in the sense of 'be nice to each other', that's *Sanskriti*. Being nasty or brutal is not.

Sanskriti kept its name in the end, luckily, and if we may add, luckily for all those who care about fighting hatred and discrimination too—no one would ever take their concerns seriously again otherwise.

This was not an aberration. This was not some "loony left-wing PC campaign", as people sometimes like to call such protests. It was a sincere, and in principle, commendable effort to fight social hatred that somehow lost its way when it came to Hindus. This is the stark absurdity that confronts Hinduism today.

There is a *lot* of talk going on about Hindus and Hinduism around the world that actually has very little to do with the realities of Hindus and Hinduism.

***

The Economist, a magazine so giddy about its urgency that it refers to itself as a 'newspaper' and not a 'magazine', describes the sacred Shiva Lingam at Amarnath as a "penis-shaped lump of ice".

The Onion, another magazine like the one above, publishes a bizarre, violently pornographic cartoon of Ganesha amidst an orgy of saints and deities of various faiths. It is presumably a statement against the protests ignited by a YouTube movie offensive to Muslims. What Gautama or Ganesha had to do with that, we do not know. It's an American magazine, by the way, the country whose government took forever to figure out that the cow-protecting people were their friends and not the Bin Laden-protecting regimes next door[3].

The New York Times, the paper of record, publishes several articles on and by Wendy Doniger, an American professor of Hinduism, and author of several 'magisterial' books on Hinduism. Doniger, whose work we shall look at closely later in this book,

 What we are living through right now is nothing less than a war over the fundamental validity of Hinduism.

characterizes herself as a lover of Hinduism and her critics as nasty, militant, prudish fundamentalists. In all these reports, we do not find the slightest admission of the fact that many *academics,* not militants, not prudes, find her work flawed, if not absurd. She also presents herself as the victim of an Indian law that makes it a *crime to offend Hindus* (though no such 'Hindu fundamentalist' law exists in India; the law in question pertains to all religions and was deployed in the past in most cases to criminalize perceived offences to other communities)[4].

The New York Times, of course, does not publish one opposing view of her work. Neither does *USA Today*, nor the *Washington Post*, nor the *Guardian*.

As for that BBC, that venerable beacon of veracity that generations of postcolonial Indians grew up revering, nothing much needs to be said either.

One billion people. Not one op-ed, not one letter, even.

Wendy Doniger, by the way, and as we shall see later in this book, compares the wanderings of the Vedic people to that of the cowboys who destroyed the Native Americans; and, for good measure, the Nazis during World War II[5].

***

Believe it or not, this is current academic knowledge. It is not idle talk, nor mere internet gossip. This is what is presumed to be *fact* in the institutions that declare what is knowledge and what is not. This is the sort of thing that universities, and serious news media, are saying about your Hinduism.

We Hindus stand accused.

We Hindus stand accused of being the Nazi-like conquerors of India.

We Hindus stand accused of being fundamentalists — despite having assured peace to numerous minority faiths in India for centuries, and despite having supported a secular idea of a nation even after partition. Just one example of this: India's state policy, according to the "award winning" *State of Religion Atlas*, "favors the religion of the majority and limits freedom of other religions" right up there with Saudi Arabia, Pakistan, Afghanistan and Iran[6].

We Hindus stand accused of being everything that we are not.

The truth though is that we Hindus, unfortunately, are typically too above such nonsense to be bothered, or too busy making money to be bothered too.

But in either case, this is not something that can be ignored much longer. *There is at the moment a very powerful, sustained, and unrelenting cultural and intellectual attack on Hinduism in the media and in the academy.* This is not the same thing as saying there is a worldwide Islamic and Christian conspiracy against Hinduism. We do say that though, but that remark loses sight of the friendship we enjoy with many Muslims and Christians and others, and it also forgets that this attack also increasingly comes not from devout Muslims and Christians but from sceptics angry at their own traditions and projecting that anger inappropriately onto ours (as for our own sceptics, we must recognize their valid points, but also encourage them to not get stuck in scepticism; when scepticism becomes the new orthodoxy, then we must be sceptical of that too). We must focus therefore not on political rhetoric but on the specificities of an intellectual position, and that is what the first part of this book does.

However, before we do so, we need to consider the possible consequences of ignoring it. I understand that is not quite a Hindu thing, or a cool thing these days in general, to be too hung up on arguments about religion. We would have probably been the last people to be doing so. There is a temptation no doubt, to ignore it. Hinduism, after all, is not going to vanish. The United States and many other countries where Hindus live respect our rights. Humanity is now in an age in which most countries respect our freedom to our own faith as a basic human right. That is what gives us our security, the rule of law, and faith in God, of course.

But the threat today is more existential than we have understood it.

What if very soon we arrive at a position when our very religion, our very culture, our names, our festivals, our gods and goddesses, come to be seen as antithetical to those very same human rights? Remember, in the past, the ignorance about Hinduism could be brushed aside as merely old world prejudice or stereotyping. It was openly expressed as religious or racial rivalry. It was ugly but at least honest. But what we face today is extremely devious, and dangerous. The attack on Hinduism today comes not from those who openly differ with us on religious grounds, but through a very ingenuous device: they say they are not against Hinduism, but only against Hindu extremism. Most Hindus are against extremism too, and would have probably been happy to agree with them, if only their position had been really against extremism alone. *But virtually every book, article, and argument made by the world's supposedly leading, important, and celebrated intellectuals today says the same thing: in the name of criticizing Hindu extremism, they savage the entirety of our religion.* If they are not challenged, intellectually and culturally, soon our names, gods, goddesses, festivals, sacred scriptures, virtually everything that makes us who we are, will be defined by them as something that it is not.

Maybe a day will come when we will feel ashamed to bear our own names again, or worship our own gods and goddesses, freely. Maybe a day will come when *Shiva's* trident can be legally interpreted as a weapon, or a *Lingabhishekham* at our temples banned as a primitive act of sexual worship.

Maybe a day will even come when even our breathing is deemed oppressive because it is saying *'soham'* and invoking the swan of Goddess *Saraswathi*!

That last example might seem extreme, but the fact is that we almost lost a word like *'Sanskriti'*. We might lose a lot more too, if we do not recognize this.

What we are living through right now is nothing less than a war over the fundamental validity of Hinduism.

And this war is cloaked in the very language that guarantees us our rights today; that of freedom, equality, democracy and justice.

It maintains one shrill, moribund, position: *if you are not with us*, you are a fundamentalist. *If you say our work is flawed and ignorant*, you are a fundamentalist.

But if the kind of things that they write about Hindus as truth were written about women, blacks, gays, Muslims, or any other community today, they would be laughed out of their offices for their bizarre 18th century racism.

But the ignorance against Hinduism is not a joke.

It has consequences.

***

Remember this:

Primed to denigrate Hindu life, the papers of prestige will not report the truth, even if it is so harsh that it hurts their own people.

Pakistani terrorists massacre Indians, Americans, Israelis, and others on 26/11/2008. Leading US newspapers like the *New York*

 > Hinduism at this moment remains bereft of a hand with which to write its own story.

Times and *LA Times* publish several op-ed pieces that blame India's policy on Kashmir, the rise of "Hindu extremism", and the appalling state of poverty among Muslims in India. There are at best only three op-eds that name the then un-nameable mastermind[7].

We know it was not poverty that caused a massacre. We know it wasn't some romantic Robin Hood justice of poor Muslims fighting back against rich Hindus. No, the victims at the Chatrapati Shivaji Terminus were poor, small, thin, human beings; fathers and brothers and mothers. They came to work that day so their children could eat the next day. They spent their bodies day after day to earn no more money perhaps than the cost of one bullet that would take their lives.

The day the op-ed pundits proclaimed that massacre as a triumph of human rights and social justice against Hindutva and India was the day they lost all moral and intellectual virtue.

No writer with million dollar advances and human rights and free speech awards wrote about what those bullets did to those poor bodies.

They did write, copiously, about one pompous thug among one billion Hindus who once boasted about killing people in Gujarat though. And they wrote, in vivid detail, about a pregnant woman whose baby was ripped out of her womb by a sword (an image, it may be noted, used by professional propagandists to start wars at least twice in the past century)[8].

***

Hinduphobia is more dangerous than any other ideology in today's civilization in some ways.

Racism, Fundamentalism, Sexism, these are dangerous, no doubt, and exist; but these are recognizable. People will know to get outraged, if a Muslim is detained unfairly in America or discriminated against in India, say.

But a massacre against Hindus does not seem to get the slightest reaction in the world press; except to perhaps say: 'Let's hope the Hindu fundamentalists now don't go on a backlash!'

But a Hindu does not feel bad only for his losses; he also sees the pain of those who suffered, the Jews, the Muslims, the Christians, everyone.

A Hindu fights Hinduphobia because doing so is the only way to save them, and to save ourselves. Our universalism is like that. We know that the ignorance that hurts us also hurts others, in different ways.

***

Hinduphobia is not a quirk or an individual stereotype that afflicts some individuals. It is a systematic distortion in human thought that serves to distract the world from the cruelty and the needlessness of suffering, not just Hindu, but all human and non-human suffering too.

It exists not so much in the indifferent mind of the average world citizen today, the American, or Muslim, or Chinese, but in the upper echelons of the institutions that define the world and its people today; the media, and the academy.

It is there that we must begin our cure.

And it won't be easy, because Hinduphobia has five hundred years of privilege that gives it a monopoly on the press and the academy, and a tremendous influence over our own postcolonial educational system and intellectual class as well.

But the time for change has come. We have a millennia-old streak of kindness finessed into intelligence. With the right determination, if all of us decide that this is important, that Hinduphobia needs to end, we can achieve what we want. We can, and we must, show those afflicted by Hinduphobia that they are not saving anybody from Hindus with their ignorance and lies. Instead, we must reveal to them how their misinformed obduracy has made them the last line of resistance between today's Hinduism and tomorrow's promise of a better world for not just Hindus, but indeed, all of this world.

We will break their fear. We will break whatever holds them, and us, back from something as simple as decency, honesty, and indeed, kindness to all.

***

How should we do this?

Forwarding emails proclaiming our ancient greatness and saying our ancient rishis were advanced missile designers will not save us.

Liking and Sharing stuff on Facebook alone will not save us.

Going to temples and doing *pujas* alone will not save us.

Sending our children to Hindu Sunday school alone will not save us.

Making our children memorize *mantras* without enjoying their meaning will not save us.

Mastering math and science and getting jobs and making lots of money will not save us (it will help though, so don't neglect them!)

Bollywood fashions and pop Hindu *bhajans* might be fun, but will not save us.

 We are not rearming Hinduism really unless we are rearming our hearts with something like kindness, and love.

And a word for those of us who already know we face an existential challenge and don't need to be convinced:

Blaming Christians and Muslims will not save us either. In fact, it is counterproductive and un-Hindu. It is true we may be fed up with pseudo-secularism. But we cannot forget that we invented secularism in the sense of respect for all faiths long before other lands had even figured out such a thing was possible. We must find our strength in that once more. After all, when Hinduphobia is conquered, and the academy resumes its pursuit of truth, historians might find one day that it wasn't just the zero and numerals that went West from ancient India, but its many humanistic ideals too. It is surely more than a coincidence that they got over their dark ages and had their Enlightenment just around the time they met us, but we don't hear much about that at all. The old Eurocentric paradigm is changing though. It has just about started to acknowledge that much of its genius was stimulated by its contact with the Arab and Islamic civilization. In time, when Hindu scholars, writers, and informed critics of Hinduphobia find their voice, we might help push the paradigm even further. A prosperous India led by a restored philosophical vision is essential for that. And we are making it happen.

***

Like the iconic sculpture of *Lakshmi-Narasimha* from the ruins of Vijayanagara that you see on the cover of this book, Hinduism at this moment remains bereft of a hand with which to write its own story. But the important thing to remember is this. While they may have broken his hands, they still could not manage to put out the fire in the Lion-God's eyes.

Jwala Mukhayanamaha.

The Fire Faced One. The *Volcano* Faced One!

For Hinduism to survive this moment, as it has survived many other moments in the past, including determined efforts in the past by two powerful imperialist forces to destroy it (and we must reiterate that we do not have a problem philosophically with the spiritual aspects of Islam or Christianity, much less with Muslims or Christians, our critique is only of the imperialism that came with some of them in the past), we need to do two things:

First, we must turn to our Gods and Goddesses in prayer, and in a spirit of devotion and surrender. Our prayer though must be noble as their ideals. We must just remember that this is not about us in a selfish sense. It is not about our pride or egos. Standing up as Hindus is to stand up only for whatever goodness, kindness, wisdom and love, for all beings, that our gods have stood for. Standing up for Hinduism can be about *raudra*, but not *krodha*.

Second, we must act. We must assume responsibility for the future of our children, the legacy of our ancestors, and most of all, in the spirit of vasudaiva kutumbakam, the future of the world (and we really must take back this beautiful ideal from its rather superficial use of late). Saving Hinduism cannot be truly Hindu in spirit if it is also not equally about saving not just Hindus, but the whole world. That is the way it has always been. Hinduism after all has never been about us or them; but only about us and them, and that 'them' includes not just people of other nations or religions, but also those living beings of different species too. We must restore Hinduism not just for the sake of Hindus, but for all living beings in this world, for the sake of all nature. Though we are not in the business of saving anything or anyone against their will, we can't help our kindness when we see destructiveness, and self-destructiveness.

Today's global, educated, and assertive Hindus are in a position now to do what that half-failed project of global modernity has been struggling to do for so many centuries now: give the world the cultural resources, indeed, the intelligence of nature it has forgotten, so that it may understand universalism and freedom, those great ideals of modern life, a little better. India has chosen prosperity again. *Rearming Hinduism*, recognizing its vastness of vision and heart, can help us move the conversation beyond the clichés of the political Right and the Left; after all, the Right in India seems to say the right things about Hinduism (such as respect for cows) but sometimes for the wrong reasons (attacking whole communities over them) and the Left seems to have the right reasons (such as concern for the poor and oppressed) but seems to be all wrong about Hinduism (as we will see in this book). *Rearming Hinduism* has to be a first step in not only restoring Hindu thought, but also in finding a way for the world that will move our present models for prosperity and growth into new ways of living in and with nature rather than at great cost to it.

***

This book begins with an outline of the key assumptions in today's academic Hinduphobia and offers a critical response to them. It might sound very academic at times, but it is not written strictly for an academic readership. My intention is to convey to a wider audience today what exactly academic writers, particularly those in what is called the critical tradition, are trying to do — and why they have failed enormously in their treatment of Hinduism. My approach is not to speculate on their intentions, or on possible conspiracies, but merely to use my tools as a media and cultural studies scholar to identify the myths in academia and commonsense that must be addressed not only by Hindus but by anyone who cares about humanity and nature.

I focus on Wendy Doniger's controversial *The Hindus: An Alternative History* as an example of Hinduphobic historiography somewhat more than others because this book, more than any other, now defines current thinking in academic and media circles about Hinduism.

As an academic, and one who was trained in critical and postcolonial media and cultural studies, I understand, despite its jargon and jarring humour, and not without empathy, the intentions of Doniger's book. I will however, show that this book does not live up to its own stated intentions either, and is merely a part of a massive, pernicious, and un-examined ideology prevalent in academia today.

My concern in *Rearming Hinduism* is with this ideology, and not necessarily with asserting another history of Hinduism. It is too vast a subject for us, or at least for me, to attempt at this time. I do however hope to prepare the ground for such work for others to do in the future by expanding the critique of the present historiography (how we speak about history), which I maintain, is a profoundly Hinduphobic one. And this Hinduphobia is not simply about hostility to Hindus emanating from zealous individuals. It is part of a deeper, unexamined prejudice that remains pervasive in today's supposedly scientific theories about the world against some of the things Hinduism has been deeply engaged with, such as animals, nature, and life in general. We cannot address Hinduphobic historiography, in other words, unless we also critique speciesist and social-Darwinist biases in today's commonsense about our past. Just for the record, our view of animals in this book will be very different from the rather bizarre, metaphoric, and anthropocentric treatment they get in Doniger's book.

Since this book believes that a history of Hinduism cannot ignore the question of what the divine means to Hindu, I offer in the second part an 'alternative' vision of sorts about Hinduism not so much as an exhaustive history of Hinduism but merely as an example of how one devout Hindu sees hope for humanity in the richness of Hindu thought. I present this part in a more personal and devotional tone rather than an academic one, and it is perhaps best read not as argument but simply as a set of thoughts, perhaps to be taken in and reflected upon in small pieces, about what it means to be human as reflected in the ideals and stories of Hinduism.

It is my hope that this book will be of interest not only to Hindus who wish to see a better understanding of their life emerge in today's world, but also to everyone who cares about things like humanity, dignity, peace, non-violence, truth, and indeed, love for all beings in this world again.

We are not rearming Hinduism really unless we are rearming our hearts with something like kindness, and love.

Mama dehi karaavalambam.

Grant us please, the refuge of Your hands[9].

***

Part 1

DESA-KALA-DOSHA

The Ideologies of Hinduphobia

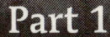

 There is no sense in the commonsense today about what is Hinduism and what is Hindu fundamentalism.

Chapter 1

THE ACADEMIC MAYA SABHA

How Academia Lost Sight of Hinduism

There is something rotten in academia.

There is something rotten in the media.

There is something rotten in the paradigm.

There is no sense in the commonsense today about what is Hinduism and what is Hindu fundamentalism.

The challenge that Hinduism faces today comes not from governments or armies, but essentially in the sphere of culture; from two institutions, academia, and the media. Modern academia and the mass media. Hardly one hundred years old. Yet, the ideas in each have become tremendously influential around the world. So influential, pervasive, and normative, that unless we learn how to question them, and how they tell the story about the world, we will forget who we really were altogether.

***

There are three things going on with the *discourse* about Hinduism today.

The predominant story, in the sense of the one which gets the most authority, visibility, prestige, and even moral urgency, is the one which comes from the critical academic tradition; the left-secular position; the one which narrates 'alternative' histories and promises subaltern recuperations. It might seem odd that something with 'subaltern' in it is actually dominant. But this is the position that is published, exclusively, in the *New York Times*, *The Guardian*, the liberal beacons — and just for the record, there is no equivalent Hindu-conservative view published in conservative Western newspapers either. Hinduphobia comes from Left and Right in the US; an achievement in itself, for there is probably no other issue on which Left and Right agree in Western discourse except on bashing Hinduism. This is the position that is published, if not entirely without challenge, in elite circles in India too.

The second trend is the *allegedly* dominant one, the hegemonic one against which the critical-subaltern heroics of the first discourse are positioned. This is an emerging civilizational discourse about Hinduism. This discourse includes the way modern Hindus are talking about their religion, culture, and history these days; both in a semi-scholarly fashion, and also in their pop cultural imagination. It is however described by its critics as Hindu nationalism, extremism, fascism or fundamentalism (not to mention internet Hindutva). It may share some assumptions with the arguments of Hindu nationalist parties, but it is much bigger than any political agenda. It includes, as we know, virtually every Indian you and I know, the doctor, engineer, or nice neighbour. No, they are not secretly plotting to take over the world and convert non-Hindus to Hinduism. Some of them might at worst rant and rave against Muslims and Christians on the internet, but they will not do worse than ranting. We must note though that they are angry. They are frustrated. They see only hypocrisy in the secular left. Their ideas are largely about finding a rational, meaningful story about themselves in the modern, global world; they seek a national narrative because, as we shall see in a moment, what they got everywhere was starkly absurd. They seek a civilizational mirror. Some of their words are extreme, ugly; and in India, some of their actions have been aggressive. But whatever this discourse is, it is not dominant. It does not exist in American textbooks. It does not exist even in Indian textbooks for that matter. It does not get a guest op-ed, or even a letter, in the *New York Times*. It just exists as a strawman to the people who do.

Then there is the third trend, which is rarely named. It is invisible. It has become so naturalized that it appears normal. It has become virtually coterminous with the first trend. Academics do not even realize what it is. Academics, with a straight face, presumably, go and study a movie like *Slumdog Millionaire*, with all its caricatured Hollywood hoax Hindu jargon about fate, its Hindu villains oppressing poor little Muslim boys, and describe it as enforcing Hinduness on us. Believe it or not. That is how blind academia is today to its most pernicious prejudice. This, simply, is Hinduphobia[1].

Our goal in this book is to name it, expose it, and demolish it.

***

Hinduism may be very ancient, but first, we must remember that what we are unpacking is not Hinduism itself, but the discourse *about* Hinduism.

We must understand therefore the process by which a particular set of ideas, assumptions, and stereotypes came to colour the stories about Hinduism in the modern world. We must understand, in particular, the history of thought in academia, in the humanities and social sciences, and how the peculiarities, politics, and sometimes, even the promises of hope in these fields has distorted and suppressed the truth about Hinduism.

This is important. The impasse we face today cannot be overcome if we continue to talk past each other. Hindus today are

> We are not without intellects, writers and voices. We are not lacking in vision, or will.

getting concerned about what scholars in fields that Indians have typically not flocked to, like history and cultural studies, are saying about their religion and them. Hindus want to know why there seems to be such a fantastic chasm dividing their commonsense understanding of their world from what some of the academic experts of Hinduism say their religion is like. It is more than a mere lack of communication, that much we cannot pretend. For an ordinary Hindu, the views of the academic expert, the renowned writer, the literary critic, and the crusading journalist today all seem to be saying the same hypocritical, contradictory thing:

There is really no religion called Hinduism; it was invented by the British and the Brahmins only in the 19th century[2].

And now, the contradiction:

Hinduism is responsible for the caste-system, in fact the two are identical. Hinduism is responsible for patriarchy and oppression of women. In fact, Hinduism was full of violence until Buddhism, Islam, and Christianity somehow civilized it.

And before we forget, Hinduism isn't an Indian religion. The Hindus were invaders of India.

These bizarre ideas are a short, but by no means unrepresentative summary of current academic, literary, and journalistic understanding of Hinduism and Hindu history.

Naturally, any Hindu with half a brain — as the saying goes — realizes this is not right. And any Hindu with half a decent dial-up speed takes his angst to the internet.

We hit out at the proponents of these theories with the limited time, vocabulary, and knowledge, and of course, media access that we have. We call them fascists and communists, not realizing that these are proud communist intellectuals, and pride themselves on being the ideological opposites of fascists. We blame their religions. We respond to the obvious idiosyncrasies and hypocrisies of their position, but do not realize that they have placed us where they want us in the debate. They tarnish us as extremists, lunatics, prudes and censors.

But what they have to realize, sooner or later, is that we are not without intellects, writers and voices. We are not lacking in vision, or will. We may be from the political right of the spectrum, we may not be from the right. It does not matter. We will speak as Hindus, and we will speak as truth demands of us that it be spoken.

The truth that we must recognize first of all is that academic Hinduphobia is not about a personal prejudice. It is an academic formation rooted in a broader, deeper political reality that goes beyond simply Hindus and Muslims and Christians. Academia, in its present form, gives us some tools to expose this, but then in time, Hinduism must also inform academia and take it beyond, well beyond where it stands today. *When Hindu thought truly informs the social sciences and humanities, it will revolutionize knowledge, humanity, and indeed the future of the world itself.*

That is what we must aim for. Not just a better press in the short term.

***

A note on objectivity, identity, and method in the social sciences[3]:

If you are a scientist, or doctor, or engineer, you may wonder how one can be 'religious' and scientific about the same thing at the same time. We are taught, after all, that being scientific means being objective, and being objective is understood to be essentially not being subjective; not looking at the world as a human being, but as an impersonal observer. In the physical world, in physics and chemistry perhaps, this works fine. In a few centuries, the scientific method has revealed how everything works and has made possible the fantastic (and sometimes foolish) technological leaps of our time. In the human world, in the social sciences, objectivity is a more tricky issue.

More than that, it is a historical issue, as in we can see how the definition of objectivity and truth has changed over the decades. And it is also a political issue. We must understand this history to understand how and why today's academic experts see themselves as heroic 'alternative' visionaries and liberators — before we demonstrate the fact that they are not.

From their inception in the early 20th century and until the late 1960s, the social sciences prided themselves on objectivity. Enchanted by science, psychologists, anthropologists, historians, and others proceeded to systematically and seemingly objectively write their accounts of human life, past and present. Some of that scholarship remains truly useful, important, and one might, say, objective too. But a great deal of social science research from that period now seems strikingly biased to us, in retrospect. Some social scientists were not objective at all, but blatantly racist, imperialist, and sexist. They measured head-shapes of people not like them (not white, simply put) and compared them to those of chimps, to 'prove' that they were of superior character and intelligence. They administered preposterous survey questionnaires to poor immigrants and proceeded to interpret their lack of knowledge of American customs as low IQ. And in the case of Hinduism and Hindus, they did pretty much whatever they wanted to do; mistranslating our sacred texts, concocting preposterous racial theories, and getting away with it because they were the masters of the world in those days, and of course, they had some powerful claims at being objective (if they agreed with each other on rules

> Hinduphobia came hard, from the Left and from the Right.

they had made up with each other, then it was deemed objective, that was it). What they were oblivious about was their privilege, and how their privilege disguised their own strange prejudices about Hindus, which were mostly of a soul-saving, if not a literally head-measuring, sort. They eased their missionary-induced biases into academic respectability without recognizing the clear power difference that gave them authority to speak about and over the 'other' without reciprocity. Simply put, academic traditions of objectivity like peer review meant nothing in those days because the racism and colonialism of the time excluded Hindus from being 'peers' who could shape a field of study supposedly about themselves.

In the 1960s and 1970s, academia went through an upheaval of sorts. The old pretense at objectivity and universal knowledge was broken; or to use the language of those who did the breaking, the hegemony was challenged. It was the beginning of the leftist takeover of the academy and the social sciences, and in the beginning, it was probably a good thing. Marxism, third-worldism, feminism, and many other positions emerged roaring into academia. They named the old 'objective' position of the social sciences as what it really was; it was not really objective or universal knowledge, but merely the biases and views of specific groups of people; they were mostly of European descent, and they were mostly male, so they were rather rudely called 'dead white males' (this phrase will come back in the Hindu context shortly in a

You had to leave five thousand years of your vast wisdom outside the door

misplaced form as we shall see). Universities realized that they couldn't teach courses on literature where only 'dead white male' authors like Shakespeare were studied, for example. Many voices established themselves in academics, and in time, in the media, and the culture at large too. Women's studies departments, ethnic studies departments, all became a part of university life. The good part of all this was that no one was getting their heads measured to be labeled as stupid any more. Diversity and empowerment had truly come to many more people and communities now.

The bad part of it was that diversity and empowerment also became a fashion. Though in a way it was more objective to speak as who one was rather than pretend to be above one's subjectivity, history, and identity, the nature of modern bureaucracies (which universities too are at some level), turned the pursuit of intellectual inquiry into a mere calculus of good and bad identities. Truth almost became irrelevant, with everything becoming relativized. Everything now was simply an opinion, with the curriculum only encouraging us to celebrate some opinions and condemn some on the basis of identities and labels rather argument and reason. It is a phenomenon that may be described as postmodernism. Whether it was truly past modernism or not, whatever its good intentions and high concepts, as far as Hindus were concerned, we ended up on the wrong side of its clichés.

We were the 'others' as far as mainstream academics went in the old days. Then, when all the 'others' got seats at the table as gendered, ethnic, and sexual minorities, we suddenly found ourselves lined up alongside the old guard, the villains of global oppression and genocide, as it were.

'Hindu' became a bad word in the university classroom. It was part of the package. If you were against racism, against sexism, against the exploitation of workers, against war, against virtually any social or political evil in the world, then somehow you had to take the package.

There was no alternative. You could not be a conservative and Hindu in academia either, because the conservative side of the academy was rooted in its old senses of racial and religious identity, and did not like Hinduism either.

Hinduphobia came hard, from the Left and from the Right. It forced Hindus in academics into a strange limbo; a continuation of the uneasy equation between successful Hindus and Euro-American elite intellectual society; you are like us, as Kennedy once told Nehru[4], Indian-Irish brothers in colonialism, maybe; but an Indian sticks out in ways Irish don't. You are told you are privileged. You are told you must now suffer the same liberal guilt white society suffers for its past. If you don't agree, you must be a racist, casteist, creationist, Hindu fundamentalist. You cannot speak, at the moment, as a Hindu intellectual.

You could be a woman, and produce knowledge as a feminist. You could be Muslim, and make claims as an Islamist historian. Your identity was somehow expected to enhance your standing as a scholar. But as a Hindu, you are deemed incapable of representing yourself, let alone objective knowledge. You are deemed incapable of being liberal, progressive, or egalitarian. You had to leave five thousand years of your vast wisdom outside the door, maybe as *karma* because they leave their shoes at ours when they enter.

We remained the last legally sanctioned, academically anointed, recipients of a very specific kind of racism and prejudice that once affected virtually the whole world but now exists only against us.

***

Orientalism is an influential idea in the humanities and social sciences. It refers to the ways in which the cultural and intellectual practices of powerful institutions (governments, universities, media), the way in which people do their jobs, simply put, the rules of the game, so to speak, end up creating a false, but powerful fantasy through which to impose their will on other people and places. In plain language, one could say, it refers to what we might call stereotypes. But in Edward Said's usage, it is far more subtle and sophisticated — using examples from literature, art, academics, and media, Said shows us how colonial rulers (mostly British and French) invented a discourse about the 'Orient' in order to justify and enable their rule and plunder of Asia and Africa. Orientalism is not an easy book to read, but a few key ideas are useful here.

Orientalism is a discourse, and a discourse is a set of statements ruled by unspoken[5] imperatives about what can be said, or not said, in that discourse. For example, in the discourse that followed 9/11 in the US, one could not say "There are no WMD's in Iraq!" in the government, think-tanks, or elite press. A discourse is backed by institutional power; it is therefore power.

Orientalism is mostly an academic discourse, though it flourishes and proliferates through very similar strategies in media, art and literature too. Said talks about the "restorative citation of antecedent authority" as a mechanism that sustains this sort of knowledge-power nexus. It is like this. For your claim to be taken as 'fact' and not merely 'opinion', it has to pass the test of peer-review and intellectual practice and be published in a scholarly journal. It will be deemed 'scholarly' only if you cite the sources who came before. What if the sources who come before were wrong? Or were brazenly sexist, racist, maybe even crazy? It doesn't matter. When you cite them, their credibility now goes up. Same logic with media stereotypes too — if Hollywood makes an India movie, it has to have poverty, snakes, weirdness; it doesn't have to look like how India looks, it only has to look like how Hollywood's India-movies look!

Orientalism about India and Hinduism has proved remarkably resilient.

In its early phase, say, from the 1800s till the 1940s, Orientalism about Hinduism was fuelled by the political interests of colonization, proselytization and the ideology of the 'civilizing mission'. Western writers, scholars, artists and politicians conjured up a morbid and false fantasy about Hinduism as a violent, superstitious, and barbaric religion, and its people as evolutionary inferiors. And since India was a colony, at least some Indians accepted at least some part of this ideology (via the policy of Anglocentric education, the Macaulay Minute). A typical example from this period was the book *Mother India*.

In the second phase, which we might call the early postcolonial/Cold War phase, academia moved slightly beyond the old, blatant stereotypes, but nonetheless retained them implicitly in new theories. From the 1950s till about the 1980s, Hinduism figured[6], negatively, if quietly, in American Cold War calculations which computed consciously in favour of Islamic Pakistan against Hindu India (Christian American leaders saw Islamic Generals as trusty allies over non-violent, vegetarian Hindus). Hinduism also figured in theories about why India was poor, often in terms like the 'Hindu rate of growth'. This phase, though, was profoundly important in India, where under the auspices of Nehruvian secularism, a broad indifference to Hinduism got set in place in academia, and also in the media and intellectual classes. Simply put, independent India did not see it fit to make any social investment in Hinduism as an intellectual or philosophical resource for its citizens, and the schoolchildren of independent India too did not acquire any more insight into their own religion and heritage beyond token heritage capsules.

In the present phase, Hinduphobic orientalism has become more subtle. After all, this is an age in which even lay audiences can call out a movie for being racist, sexist, or stereotypical (except *Slumdog Millionaire*, of course). The way orientalism figures against Hindus today is not so much through an attack on their alleged inferiority (as the colonial and cold war phases did) but through the fantasy of their alleged oppressiveness. With margins and underdogs suddenly becoming cool, academia and popular culture abruptly reconfigured Hindus in their view to go directly from having been losers and weaklings to the complete opposite. The Hindu, in today's academia and pop culture stereotype, is a vile, racist[7], macho, sexist, oppressor. Ironically, the same activists and academics who now denounce Hinduism were probably once hippy seekers who turned to Eastern culture and religion in the 1960s as a way of rebellion against the racist, classist, and sexist structures of Western industrial society. Their rise to academic prominence should have marked the beginning of the end for the old stereotypes about Hindus and Hinduism. But nearly fifty years after the rise of cultural studies, postcolonial studies, ethnic studies, South Asian studies, diaspora studies, and their great ideals of giving voice to previously marginalized communities, Hindus find themselves even more silenced.

In many ways, the Hinduphobia that pervades academia and media today is a classic case of orientalism. Unfortunately, the same political-intellectual community that is quick to recognize orientalism against virtually any other group of people has failed to do so when it comes to Hindus. Instead, through a grotesque evasion of political and historical reality, the scholarly consensus on Hinduism has turned around and made Hinduism seem guilty of orientalizing itself! It is the cornerstone of all the myths that allow the academic Left to be one way with injustice, untruth, and oppression everywhere, and then another way with Hindus and India. It quietly equates the power of Hindus in India with the power that colonial Britain, France and later the United States had over the world and all its races. It quietly asserts a cut and paste model of critique from the West to India.

It claims Hindus have been doing to India what whites did to Native Americans, blacks and others.

It claims Brahmins have the same role in Hinduism that the church did in the rise of European colonialism.

On these delusions, it proceeds to proclaim, publish and pontificate its 'alternative' histories of Hinduism. In the next chapter, we will see why this 'alternative' is no alternative at all, but merely the dominant Hinduphobic world-story concealing itself now under the noble ideal of empowering the marginalized voice in history.

***

Secularists are as capable of being clichéd and reactionary these days as the conservatives they rail against.

Chapter 2

THE MYTH OF AN 'ALTERNATIVE HISTORY'

Wendy Doniger's book is the same old Mainstream, Hinduphobic Orientalist History

Wendy Doniger's *The Hindus: An Alternative History*, by virtue of its celebrated 'banned book' status (technically though, it wasn't 'banned', but withdrawn by its publisher as part of an out of court settlement, and far from being rendered invisible, it has since landed in what its author calls "single digit heaven" on sales rankings) and not by any intrinsic virtue as such, is the book that has defined, and will continue to define Hinduism for several years now unless the voices of reason and truth that are being presently excluded persist, and succeed, in exposing the extreme distortions this book espouses.

Firstly, as a fellow academic, I extend the courtesy of a fair reading and summary of Professor Doniger's book—though we must note again that in none of her numerous op-eds and interviews following the well-publicized controversy about her book has she acknowledged any criticism of her work from peers and reasonable readers (she mainly quotes what sound like anonymous internet trolls angry at her). Anyway, for our part, we remain who we are, and we stand respectful of truth. The truth is that she, and her supporters, *believe,* however incredible it may seem to Hindus today, that they are standing up for a liberal view of Hindu history that recognizes the contributions of the 'margins' over a dominant, hegemonic, mainstream view of Hindu history that doesn't.

We must acknowledge therefore what exactly our response to this position will be, because secularists are as capable of being clichéd and reactionary these days as the conservatives they rail against — we must emphasize that *we are not against* free speech, even Professor Doniger's, and we are not against liberal values. We must not succumb to identity-slogans (even if it seems that's what academics do these days with all their *you-bad-Hindu* talk!). We have all learned much from Western and non-Hindu observers of Hinduism. We welcome scholarship. But we cannot pretend that a grave, brazen error should go uncorrected simply because *some* Hindus react angrily to such errors. We cannot also continue to ignore the nature of the privilege, based on nationality, race, and class that insulates such errors from our sincere effort to correct them. We cannot also ignore the harmfulness that such ignorance invariably breeds towards innocent people far removed from the world of expensive hardback English-medium books too (and the harmfulness is not an exaggeration; Doniger's book may be a typical postmodern leftist argument, but it also appears to be popular among right-wing racial and religious supremacists in the West for its attacks on Hinduism).

***

The Hindus: An Alternative History, according to its author, brings to light a narrative "alternative" to "the one" based on famous Sanskrit texts. It presumes, in other words, that there is a dominant narrative about Hindu history; sort of like how world-history used to have a dominant narrative written from a Eurocentric perspective. For example, the dominant narrative about American history used to talk about how Columbus 'discovered' America, and glorified the 'scientific curiosity' that sparked the voyages of noble 'explorers' like him. This was a well-established dominant narrative, taught in history books in school, and repeated endlessly in popular culture until it became (and still is, to some extent) a part of commonsense. But in recent times, the dominant narrative has been rightly challenged. Younger Americans are now exposed to other points of view. They realize, for example, that the dominant narrative only saw it from a settler perspective, and that the Native American view was very different. Books like Howard Zinn's *A People's History of the United States* are widely read in colleges, and celebrate the role of slaves, women, workers and other marginal figures not usually addressed in mainstream histories[1]. *The Hindus*, presumably, seeks to do something along the same lines.

If that is the intention, we could not fault it for trying to be more inclusive, pluralistic, and the like. Since the 1980s, when a series of political calculations and missteps in India led to the rise of an aggressive Hindu nationalist movement, there has been anger among Hindus about the place of Muslims in India. In a rather unimaginative, un-Indian, and un-Hindu manner, some Hindus began to go around thinking and saying Muslims have no place in India, and ought to go to Pakistan since that was their nation (and we might add; there are many more such nativisms in India, almost every group seems to want someone else to go away, North Indians, South Indians, Hindus, Muslims; the only place in India though where a mass-expulsion has taken place recently is in Kashmir; and it was the Hindus who were expelled). All the same, we can agree that telling neighbours to go away is distasteful.

Some Hindus also began to take things rather literally about their faith, and lose sight of the richness of Hinduism and its diversity; not necessarily because they were fundamentalists, but mostly because they did not know better. A Hindu who knows two Indian languages or has lived in two different regions, for example, might know a little more about Hinduism's diversity than say a Hindu who knows only one. Whatever the reasons for these changes, in an age when religious fundamentalism seemed to be a growing problem worldwide, it seemed to many liberal observers and scholars that Hinduism was turning into full-blown fascism. That is what they said, and that is the concern that Doniger's book to tries to address. This much, we can grant.

And this much, we can say: if Doniger, or any of these writers and scholars, accurately and honestly understood the differences between Hinduism, Hindu nationalism, and Hindu extremism ('Hindu fundamentalism' is, frankly, a misnomer; for there has not been neither a centralized nor even an institutionalized push toward a literal, fundamentalist reading of the texts in Hindu history), then there would not have been a problem today. Their work would not have been what we call these days an 'Epic Fail'.

The trouble is that the truth is so obvious to everyone today, except it seems to those who are steeped in this Hinduphobia masquerading as progressive criticism.

***

So let us see then, what the 'dominant narrative' about Indian history says. Let us recall what our history textbooks taught us about Hinduism when we were growing up in India.

This is the Mainstream History, as we learned it in school (India):

- Indian history begins with the Indus Valley Civilization (which is not Hindu).
- Hinduism begins with the Aryan Invasion bringing Vedic Religion of Sacrifice.
- Hinduism is full of violent animal sacrifice until Buddhism reforms it.
- There is a brief Golden Age for Hinduism in which art and culture 'flourishes', and the epic-poems *The Ramayana* and *Mahabharatha* are composed.
- There are Islamic invasions, but the Mughals bring harmony under Akbar.
- The British colonize India; Hinduism is reformed.

> *How can this be an 'alternative' when its claims are the same as the dominant narrative?*

- Gandhi and Nehru free us. We proclaim ourselves a sovereign, socialist, secular, democratic republic, about which we read more in Civics class.

Let us also look at Mainstream History, as it is taught to American school children, from a California textbook:

- Indian history begins with the Indus Valley Civilization (which is not Hindu).
- Hinduism begins with the Aryan Invasion bringing Vedic Religion of Sacrifice.
- Hinduism is full of violent animal sacrifice until Buddhism reforms it.
- The epic-poems *The Ramayana* and *Mahabharatha* are composed. They have talking monkeys and bears and Hindus primitively animal-worship them. They also have the holiest text of Hindus, the *Gita*, which tells Hindus to do their caste-duty and war.

Now, let us look at the outline of the 'alternative' history proposed in Wendy Doniger's book:

- The Indus Valley Civilization (is not Hindu).
- Hinduism begins with the Nazi-like Aryans bringing Vedic Religion of Sacrifice.
- Hinduism is full of violent animal sacrifice until Buddhism reforms it.
- There is no real Golden Age as such for Hinduism but the Greek Invasion leads to great ideas and works of fiction

like *The Ramayana* and *Mahabharatha*. Greek women presumably inspired the fierce and independent Draupadi.
- After chapters called '*Sacrifice in the Vedas*' and '*Violence in The Mahabharatha*', at long last, we have '*Dialogue and Tolerance under the Mughals*'.
- The British colonize India; Hinduism is reformed.
- But once India is independent, without those civilizing external forces, the Hindus now become Hindutva extremists.

Which leads us then to that overwhelming question:

How can this be an 'alternative' when its claims are the same as the dominant narrative?

***

There is also another sly bit of deceit (not to mention conceit) at work in the rhetoric of heroic resistance that has erupted around Wendy Doniger's book. An 'alternative' position implies that it is a relatively powerless one, or at least one which does not have the same level of privilege and access as mainstream positions into the discourse about a subject.

Walk into your Barnes and Noble and look at the Hinduism or Eastern Religion shelf. Look at the World History or South Asia shelf. In the highly competitive world of international publishing and book retailing, the presence of a title before possible readers represents a tremendous amount of privilege, one that perhaps 99% of authors do not have. It is easy to say anyone can publish on the internet; but the fact remains that there is a system of privilege and reward in the cultural and intellectual world. This 'alternative' history of Hinduism is at the top of the heap. Its author's books dominate the shelf, and dominate the press coverage. In a normal world, if there were ten titles written by 'Hindu right-wing extremists' on the shelf, then, an 'alternative' would have truly been an *alternative* and worthy of the respect that term brings.

Crying persecution from the privileged comfort of the top ranks of an ivory-tower is like the character in the old novel *The Red Badge of Courage*. At least in fiction, he had a twinge of conscience.

***

This is the reality of power and privilege. Your *London Review of Books*, your *New York Times*, your NPR and BBC, will celebrate an 'alternative' history but not once stop to think about the supposed 'mainstream' it is opposing. We do not hear the views of a 'mainstream' Hindu scholar of Hinduism, let alone a Hindu nationalist writer against whom this book is supposedly written, ever published in these places. On the other hand, the so-called 'alternative', by virtue of its American provenance, travels hard around the world and sells well, and displaces local voices easily. Resume your survey of the intellectual real-estate market in the world today. Look at bookstores, prestigious op-ed and review pages, and the canon of media-anointed intellectual celebrity.

In the past few years, the only people whose views on Hinduism have been heard on a worldwide scale are people who have been uniformly uninformed, if not hostile, to Hinduism. Sen, Doniger, Nussbaum, Mishra, Roy; just a handful of names all saying the same thing, really[2].

It is important to recognize this phenomenon for what it is. We end up either accepting their position in the hierarchy as something worthy because we somehow like to believe in meritocracy and assume that their exalted status is beyond question, or we end up condemning Christians and Muslims for keeping us down. There is a better way of looking at this.

Media scholars call it cultural imperialism; simply put, Hollywood outsells local film industries in virtually every country, and in the same way, academic Hollywood outsells local scholars and writers everywhere, even in India, with its supposedly Hindu fascist hegemony censoring free speech. So even if an 'alternative' historian like Wendy Doniger modestly says hers is only 'a history' and not 'the history', it doesn't matter. The privilege of her pulpit guarantees her book more than merely 'alternative' placement in bookstores, reviewers' lists, and the academic canons. Once again, look at the pecking order of publishing. This is the book that will define Hinduism now in the circles of prestige.

***

Finally, a courtesy, once again for what Doniger, Nussbaum, Sen and others have been trying to do here. We understand, the 'alternative' being proposed here is not to the really dominant narrative of Indian history textbooks as they exist or to the California history textbooks, but to the dominant, hegemonic, fascist *Hindutva* version of history — the one that the Hindu fascist forces have been *trying* to ram down all our throats now since the 1990s.

The fact remains that the Hindutva versions of history, frankly, are not the mainstream, official, schoolbook history in India too, notwithstanding the occasional attempts to 'saffronize' history. The assertions of 'saffron' history are often an inadequate, sometimes self-defeating attempt to respond to a glaring hole in the modern Hindu imagination. But even if we grant that there are some absurd and extreme examples in Hindutva pamphleteer histories, these are barely addressed in Doniger's book. There is no summary of the views from a Hindu nationalist organization's stated position. There is little direct evidence in fact of what the supposedly Hindu nationalist historians argue. We are left to surmise, from stunningly cool phrases like 'dead male Brahmins', that there is a dominant Hindu history to this counter-narrative, and it is written by these elite, violent, cow-killing, patriarchal Brahmins, silencing the voices of women, subalterns, others, crushing the pluralism and diversity of the many tellings of the *Ramayana*, rewriting history, marching on, like Nazis on genocide (this might seem a harsh criticism to make, but one will see why, soon...).

It might be the case that some celebrated writers not only do not get Hinduism, they do not quite get Hindutva too.

What they do therefore, it appears, is to cut and paste a standard 'alternative' critique of Western historiography into South Asia, followed by a find and replace of 'dead white males' with 'dead male Brahmins'. That is an example of the sort of superficiality that stares at us from *The Hindus: An Alternative History*, from Amartya Sen's *Argumentative Indian*, from Martha Nussbaum's *The Clash Within* and from Pankaj Mishra's glorious paeans to books like this in the New York review pages. We know there is a place in the discourse on Hinduism for conservative views and for progressive views too; but these are neither. These are just fantasies.

***

A modern Hindu wonders. There is only so much one can do or say to convince one's self that the power relations between Hindus and Muslims in India, or between different caste-communities today, is similar to the power relations that existed between Nazi Germans and Jews and Gypsies, or White Settlers and Native Americans, or European Colonizers and the people of Africa, Asia, and Latin America. There is no Hindu *anschluss* in India, nor will there be one. India does not work that way. Hinduism does not work that way. There may be an element of Hindu militancy, but that cannot be wished away as long as there are other militancies in the world too.

What then is the merit of this cut and paste critique? Is the 'dead male Brahmin' indeed the equivalent of the 'dead white male'?

For one thing, every Hindu knows or believes that the two sacred epics were written not by Brahmins but by a lower-caste thief turned sage (Valmiki), and a half-caste son of a fisherman's daughter (Veda Vyasa). We know the two human-form gods we worship most, *Rama* and *Krishna*, were not Brahmins. We know there are hundreds of variations floating around of our stories, all around us; in our classrooms, in our media, in our lives, and even in our own families. We are used to our gods being as mixed up as us.

Yet, we are told, we have some dead male Brahmin hegemony in our religion that is also somehow a Hindu nationalist history that this alternative heroically contests, gets pulped over, and thereby becomes the voice of everyone who is against fundamentalism.

The truth is that we care little about purity, hegemony, or denying the rights of others to live in India. Some of us are angry, no doubt, very angry. And when terrorists blast bombs in India, again and again, some of us write angry columns and comments calling for loyalty oaths and other improper suggestions. That anger was misplaced, and for the most part, it has moved on from where it was in the 1980s and 1990s. Hindus have made a new accommodation with Muslims in India. They will argue, occasionally, thanks to the internet, in ugly and absurd forms. But they will live on, as they have for centuries.

Hindus have moved beyond the gung-ho religious nationalism of the 1980s. Hindus have moved beyond the caste equations of the centuries. Hindus have moved beyond the gender equations of the past.

***

There are three basic realities in Hinduism and Indian history that these 'alternative' myths ignore:

One, the Hindu 'mainstream' in India is not what people abroad, even the scholars, assume it to be. Eighty per cent Hindu is not the same power-bloc as an 80% white nation. Even the Hindu nationalist parties as they are called never get the majority Hindu vote. Hindus are highly diverse, politically; and demographically, in terms of language, region, caste, community and so on. So though it seems natural enough for human rights watchers and others to speak of 'Hindus killing Muslims' such a generalization is rarely accurate. Even in the case of Partition, the fact remains that it was not Tamil Hindus, or Maharashtrian Hindus, or Hindus and Muslims *everywhere* that attacked each other. It was a tragedy that played out intensely, but only in two regions, not more. What seems like national conflict is often highly local, and only interpreted in macro-political terms to suit certain narratives (such as the British intellectual-political class's *ye olde* lamentation of Indian/Hindu oppression of Pakistani/Muslim victims, seen recently in the form of Perry Anderson's essay in the *London Review of Books* that berates even that too-Hindu oppressor of Muslims, Mahatma Gandhi)[3]. Yet, oblivious to these diverse identities, commentators insist; a nativist, anti-upper-caste group's attack on a library was a 'Hindu attack'; a militant separatist movement in another country was somehow fuelled by Hinduism (the religion critic Sam Harris goes so far as to claim that Hinduism's reincarnation belief is what must have made the LTTE's suicide-bombing possible)[4].

Two, the caste issue is also highly convoluted. Western commonsense believes, after centuries of orientalist propaganda, that essentially only the West has freedom and individualism, and others don't; that we 'ethnics' are all ruled by our cultures, passions, or religions[5]. Since it is wrong to say caste has disappeared in India, we don't; and they assume their fantasies are all correct, that Hinduism goes around dictating every little bit of oppression and venality in Slumdog India. The reality though is this. And this is what liberal Hindus should feel free to speak up: one, caste discrimination is illegal in India[6] (except for affirmative action), we have a constitution, and a reasonably strong democracy, and through these institutions many once-lower castes have acquired considerable political weight and economic privilege now; two, the 'upper caste' Brahmins are not the 'upper class'; many economic and political elites today come from what may have been 'lower castes' two generations ago; three, people don't always care about caste in a religious sense, or a cultural sense; it may play out in issues like marriage, but it is on the whole, not what it was even fifty years ago. While caste remains important in politics, the fact is we do not have a system of caste apartheid in a civic sense, especially in urban India. We did not after all have rules about who could sit where on a bus unlike the USA that did so until the mid-twentieth century.

Three, we Hindus do not claim to be perfect. In fact, we are as flawed as anyone. We are not, as we are accused of being, 'exceptionalists'. We have a very human understanding of ourselves, and others. The fact is that we have lived with diversity for very long, historically speaking. Our views are cosmopolitan in some ways, and intolerant and clannish in others. However, there is an essential difference between the *social and political ideologies about other people and groups* that modern Hindus have, and the deeper, *older, ever-evolving sensibilities about the divine* that Hindus also have. For example, a modern, educated, middle class Hindu, when asked about the reason for poverty India, might respond that a poor person is poor because of population, or government corruption, or even something racial, like genetic lack in intelligence (this seems less, informally speaking, these days). These ideas come, not from Hinduism, but respectively, from Malthusian Development discourses, Neo-liberalism, and Colonial-era social Darwinism and racism, borrowed into terms of caste. They might also say *karma*, but that is about all that is Hindu in this social ideology. We need to respect this difference, because the scholarship on Hinduism and India today doesn't. That is the problem with academics, my field as a whole. We go in to study the *Ramayana* and *Mahabharatha* on TV, or how *Amar Chitra Kathas* are read[7], and we come back again and again with only one finding: they spread Hindutva and hatred for minorities (we forget, for example, that there were titles in *Amar Chitra Katha* like *Babur, Humayan, Sher Shah, Akbar, Jahangir, Shah Jahan, Noor Jahan, Razia Sultana, Chand Bibi* and others, and only lament that Aurangzeb was not given a duly sympathetic title and treatment). We only find what we look for. I do not disagree that the social ideologies are relevant, but scholars also cannot pretend that the *Mahabharatha* and *Ramayana* have nothing to do with how Hindus view the divine, with Hinduism, that is. That is the problem with Doniger's book, and with the academic discourse on Hinduism today. It is not about Hinduism as much as how Hindus as a social group may be thinking about other social groups, a bunch of modern fictions really.

The truth is that there is no Dominant Narrative in Hinduism or in Indian life of the sort that Doniger insinuates. Hinduism did not have that kind of centralizing, bureaucratic, fundamentalist power; in the past, or even in post-independence India. There is no 'mainstream' Hindu history in the market against which a heroic, resistant 'alternative' must fight to rise up and be recognized.

Or maybe, there is. It is called *The Hindus: An Alternative History*. It is the last dominance-display of a dying hegemony and we shall ease its pain, mercifully. This is 2015.

We would not have a problem with it, except if you ignore the big piece of India on which Hinduism has rested altogether.

Chapter 3

THE MYTH OF ARYAN ORIGINS

The Hindus did not invade India

There is one indefensible fantasy at the core of today's historiography: that Hindus are ancient conquerors of India, just like the medieval Muslims of Central and Western Asia, and the Christian Europeans centuries later.

No matter what the intentions behind this argument, this is still a fantasy.

Even if one wishes to disagree with the ideology of Hindu nationalism, one cannot pretend that what was, really wasn't, or what never was, really is.

Liberal Hindus, normal Hindus, when they are not being angry about being talked at and talked down to by self-proclaimed liberal secularists, would probably be the first to agree that the invasion of India by Turks and Mongols centuries ago does not justify hatred towards Muslims today. If that was the point that had to be made, the alternative historians and secularists could have made it easily, elegantly, and effectively.

But they didn't. They presume that whatever Hindus are trying to discover about their own history after centuries of distortion and confusion, is part of a Hindu nationalist conspiracy. Rather than simply agree with reality and say, yes, Islam came to India from elsewhere, but it is Indian now and let's respect that instead of dreaming about expelling Muslims to Pakistan. That is all that really needed to be done about Hindu nationalism. It was an argument in the present, about the future.

Instead, the alternative historian tells us that not only did Hinduism come to India from abroad, like Islam and Christianity later, but why, didn't you know — India itself came to India from Africa!

Wendy Doniger begins her story 50 million years ago, when a piece of land broke off from Africa and voyaged across primal oceans to smash, violently, into what is now Asia, and became India.

One could have enjoyed this as an example of a vast, epic cosmological vision. But it is only an illusion of one. It is meant to assert a didactic point. We are meant to get over the notion of Hinduism as an Indian religion. Little pieces of Africa, Samarkand and England all contributed to the mosaic of Hinduism, she notes. A lovely thought. We would not have a problem with it, except if you ignore the big piece of India on which Hinduism has rested altogether.

***

Hinduism has not typically been obsessed about origins in a geographical sense (though alternativists balk at words like 'typical' when it comes to saying something factual, normal, or true about Hinduism). We do not locate our beginning with the birth, or death, of any one founder, real, imagined, or mythologized. We do not locate our beginning with any one place on the planet, or up in the sky. We do not really have a sense of where we are from, in the sense of a piece of land. We do not locate our beginning with any kind of a diagnostic manual of debts and deaths, nor do we enforce its meaning on us through vast bureaucracies. In fact, depending on

> But in our hearts, we cannot ever think of the deeds of our gods as mere fairy-tales.

the idiosyncrasies of our parents and ourselves, we are very free to imagine our Hinduism for ourselves without fear of something bad happening at all.

Since we are accustomed to eternities in ways others cannot possibly appreciate, we deal with origins in poetic fashion.

We speak of an endless *Lingam*, a column of fire, so vast that even Vishnu and Brahma could not find its beginning and end.

We speak of Vishnu sleeping and waking, universes dissolving and being born again. We speak in millions and billions of years.

We do so not because we reject science's view of age, but only because we do not presume to place our certainties above the humility this earth and its vast history instills in us.

We speak therefore of *sanathana dharma*, the way it always is.

And we speak also of the Vedas. We say they are very old. We do not presume to locate them in time and space much more than that.

***

The arguments today about Hinduism's origins largely revolve around geography. The dominant, academically sanctioned history maintains that Hinduism began with the composition of the Vedas by a gang of violent horsemen who swept down from Central Asia into the Punjab. The less accepted history, one that naturally appeals to modern Hindus, whether they are Hindu nationalists, or just Hindus, is the idea that Hinduism was already in place in the subcontinent by the time of the Indus Valley Civilization. The difficulty in the modern Hindu mind lies in reconciling the timeline of modern world history with the more elusive chronology of religiously significant events like the birth of Rama and Krishna. Modern history after all does not record their existence.

For many decades, a typically secular compromise held; Hindus would continue to privately believe in the historical reality of the gods, especially the *avatars*, but publicly, in their exams for example, observe the established academic practice of not ever speaking *Krishna* and *Rama* as real, historical figures. We wrote, in our exams, that the *Ramayana* and *Mahabharatha* were composed at a certain time in Indian history, implying our acceptance, perhaps, that these were literary creations, and not really accounts of historical events, much less the deeds of gods. But in our hearts, we cannot ever think of the deeds of our gods as mere fairy-tales. We do not know yet what to call them, so for now we call them, respectfully, stories about our gods. We somehow feel they happened, if not literally, at least loosely. Our philosophical vision doesn't insist on a separation between the human and the divine. There were presumably some human beings whom we perceived to be *avatars*, divinity incarnate.

But their absence in history is not our main problem now, for we understand the limits of method and evidence. The problem is the assumption in historiography today about what existed before what historians call civilization, and this assumption is of course naturalized through media and popular culture as a part of our commonsense. To understand what is wrong with Hinduphobic claims about our origins, we have to also understand the assumptions in the popular story today about human origins.

The Story of Man:

Ape/Man walks out of Africa and keeps going all the way across Asia, Alaska and down the Americas till very nearly the South Pole. He is savage, hairy, violent, a hunter-gatherer. He is caked in mud and blood, and grunts and heaves his way across swamps, scratching hunting tales in caves, leaving signs of some primitive religion supposedly to deal with killing and death and fear about them. Then, after tens of thousands of years of this stuff, some civilizations form in river valleys in West Asia, and if we stretch it, okay, the furthest we could go to the East, let's say, *all the way East* to the Indus Valley (that phrase tells us the location of the geographical point of view of the unnamed narrator of this story). And then, after the fall of the Indus Valley (which was not Hindu), Hinduism arrives from up north, in the form of the horse-riding, blood-spilling, Veda-reciting Aryans. This is the story we are expected to accept blindly today.

The story of man is not quite what it seems too. There is no need to dispute its basics, such as evolution, for Hindu sensibility does not demand such a split between man and animal to sustain its conception of the divine. But there is enormous possibility for critique, for imagination, for questions about the assumptions in the way we tell our story in science today. Conventional history, with its fossils, remains, ruins and (fossilized) texts cannot tell us much more. An alternative is hard to prove, because evidence is sparse, but that does not mean an alternative cannot be imagined. That alternative is essential now in understanding Hinduism. It is not just texts, but the *sensibilities* after all that we now broadly describe as Hinduism.

How did these sensibilities arise? How did this supposed wandering hunter-gatherer turn into an advocate of *ahimsa*?

Or is it just that the hunter-gatherer lineage's ethnocentric imagination was the one that wrote the story of everyone and everything that we live in today? We shall explore this possibility in the next two chapters.

***

We Hindus, a billion of us, nearly one-fifth of humanity today, are supposedly the children of a group of violent horsemen from Europe and Central Asia who invaded India. Our Hinduism, one of the oldest unbroken, ever-adapting spiritual and cultural traditions of

> To fight Hinduphobia, we must be genuinely Hinducentric, and to be genuinely Hinducentric, we must be as universal as we can be!

celebrating non-violence, animal life, and religious diversity and pluralism in the world, is supposedly rooted in a set of holy texts that describe killing and mutilating.

Why is such an absurdly false story still being enshrined and taught as history? To some extent, we must take responsibility for our own indifference, and to some extent, we must also recognize that in the past we did not have the cultural power to contest this sort of propaganda. For several hundred years, Hindus were forced to just about survive culturally in the face of colonialism. We kept our customs, temples, and beliefs, but we could not assert the philosophies underlying them intellectually. After independence, we neglected our own history, and more or less accepted what we were given by our former masters. In more recent times, with the rise of a global Hindu middle class, we have started to become more self-aware, and assertive too. But the problem is that we still do not know what is the right answer. In the absence of careful preparation and homework, we were caught unprepared. When we went to speak for the truth, as in the case of the California textbooks controversy[1] in 2006, we got tarnished as 'creationists' and 'fundamentalists'. We cannot say, for example, that we disagree with the Aryan Invasion theory because our scriptures say Rama lived millions of years ago and therefore India was Hindu for millions of years. We will be laughed at as creationists if we do. Science has pretty much established a consensus that there were no human beings millions of years ago. We cannot take our stories, sacred and sublime as they are, as if they were literal accounts of history. We are too old, and too complex, for that.

What we should do instead, is turn the mirror of intellectual inquiry upon those who defend the indefensible now. Some of our writers have attempted to do so. The problem however is that we need to go further, beyond civilization and geography. To fight Hinduphobia, we must be genuinely Hinducentric, and to be genuinely Hinducentric, we must be as universal as we can be! It sounds paradoxical, but the answers to today's problems go beyond history, into what we call pre-history too.

***

The most obvious source of distortion in the writing of Hindu history may be described as Eurocentrism. It doesn't mean European people are all prejudiced, but something more complex. It refers to the specific point of view that emerged in a specific time and place in history, and then spread through the world due to colonization; it is not just ethnocentrism, but ethnocentrism given an army, navy, media and universities to go global and universal with[2].

The Aryan Invasion story, and many other elements of history books today, are remnants of histories written during colonial times by European colonial 'scholars'. Although some of them were admirers of the new lands they were 'discovering', most were part of a great political project, to essentially colonize the people of Asia, Africa, and the Americas. To do this, they had to convince themselves of their own superiority, and the colonized subjects' of their inferiority. They decided to give themselves a noble purpose, which they called the 'civilizing mission.' Since they had lately emerged from some very dark times (think of *Game of Thrones*) through what they called the Enlightenment, they decided the rest of the world now had to have been very dark too. So everywhere they went, they made up stories; about savages, cannibals, human-sacrifice, and the like.

But since India seemed obviously civilized to them, they came up with the theory that the Hindus were

> The elevation of the settler's point of view over that of the native's is a classic colonial trope.

probably once of their own kind, now grown dark and dull in the sun, the notorious Aryan Invasion theory. (In other places, Eurocentrism would eventually merge into even funnier explanations: think of the occasional stories we hear that the pyramids were probably built by UFOs, aliens and the like, these are denials not only of rationality, but also of the non-European civilization's claim to its own intelligence and accomplishment. Anything, rather than admit that civilization existed outside Europe and, before Europe). The Aryan Invasion story is not only a questionable claim about origins but also structures a much larger narrative about how India and Hinduism have come from the past to the present. It repeats a native/settler dichotomy again and again. In the old dominant world histories written when Eurocentrism was brazen and legal, the native was usually primitive, backward, or otherwise uncivilized, and the settler brought science, civilization, and progress. In the newer alternative histories in which Eurocentrism is less brazen but still legal, the dichotomy is softened with some sort of settler guilt while the native is elevated to a romantic 'noble savage'. In the case of Hindu histories, we find these tendencies playing out in a bizarre fashion, reflecting the academic roller-coaster move of shifting Hindus from heathens to oppressors. Doniger after all does not merely repeat the usual story of Hinduism having originated with an Aryan Invasion, but gives us a whole new set of comparisons for our ancestors as well: she writes that the Vedic urge for wandering grew into the European settlers' idea of manifest destiny over the Americas as well as the Nazi policy of annexation[3].

It was bad enough that we grew up reading in our histories that the Vedas were composed by Aryan invaders from Central Asia, but now there is an even bigger connection the alternative historian has proposed: the Hindus, it would seem, are the forerunners of the greatest act of genocide in recent history.

For a group of people who mostly stayed home and rarely conquered others, that is indeed a hefty accomplishment.

It is bizarre but not surprising given how far-fetched the Hinduphobic discourse of today will go to act out its hateful delusions. A massacre in Scandinavia, by a white supremacist, as far away from India and from Hinduism as it might get, and the secularists pounce all over the papers about his alleged admiration for Hindu nationalist ideology.

If lives weren't at stake, it would actually be very funny. In the absence of an actual singularly Hindu-perpetrated genocide in history that would actually support their delusions, today's theorists go around pinning Hindu angles on any crime they can find.

The Hindus-as-conquerors trope does not end with comparisons to this genocide. For good measure, Doniger also informs us that the Vedic "cowboys" denigrated the natives of India as "barbarians" not unlike the American cowboys who denigrated the native people of North America.

That's two genocidal comparisons now in Hindu history; one, the most intense and horrific in its execution, the other the most arrogant and widespread in its manifestation.

Nazis. Conquistadors. Hindus. Even Indiana Jones's whip would not be able to touch that.

***

The hearty tale of Hinduism being invented by wandering skull-slicing proto-Nazis instead of gentle sages meditating in the mountains and forests as we think reflects another, deeper bias. This one too is rooted in Eurocentrism, in the sense that it

> Post-independence, we persisted in perpetuating this highly culturally specific denial of our own indigenous systems of knowledge.

comes out of a colonial settler's perspective. But it goes far beyond history in its scope. By bringing in the vast temporal sweep of natural history and evolution, one can easily dismiss anyone's sense of place, home, and sovereignty. Consider the story of man as it is taught today. Any modern, educated middle-school child can look at a map and tell us, with god-like authority, how the first humans walked out of Africa, into Asia and across what is now the Bering Strait into North America, and all the way down to the Southern tip of South America. It may not be incorrect, but it is still a bit of a ploy, a Eurocentric ploy. If the dominant history held that Columbus discovered America, and the alternative story tried to assert the native American view, the ultimate settler of arguments, science, evolution, now gives us a whole new shine on the past; why, it says, the native Americans weren't really native either, they were immigrants too! The elevation of the settler's point of view over that of the native's is a classic colonial trope; after all, until recently, world history was often taught according to the terms of the 'discoverers', the European colonizers, that is. Since the settler's brutal past cannot be denied any more, in a typically postmodern relativization, we are now told that everyone is a settler, even the Native Americans.

The myth of migrants and cosmopolitanism is still a myth; we need to understand how and where it started. To some extent, it became especially fashionable since the 1980s in the writings of diasporic writers and progressive commentators. As an antidote to fundamentalism and nativism, it was obviously a welcome move, to remind ourselves that we have all, at some point, come from somewhere else, that we should not be possessive about place, nor should we dispossess others. It is a very similar move that Doniger's alternative history attempts about Hindus. The difference of course, is that Hindu nativism is not necessarily the dominant one or the only one in India, nor is the alternative that is offered to this, the myth of an ancient Hindu invasion of India, very convincing either.

Home and travel are highly subjective, and depend on perspective too. It is true that man walked out of Africa and settled the whole world thus. We must not forget the brotherly sentiment therein. Unfortunately, when we talk about a process that occurred over tens of thousands of years in the same manner as more immediate, tangible and recent invasions and colonizations whose consequences we are still living with, we no longer have perspective. We can talk about how the Americas were colonized by Native Americans before the Spanish millennia later. It does not mean the same thing at all (and we must wonder if people whose migration took place over thousands of years actually thought of themselves as migrants at all, considering they stayed 'home' wherever they were in the course of their lifetimes for the most part). All it tells us is that Eurocentrism is very, very rampant, even in the tales we weave today about the origins of the human race. Sometimes, looking at ourselves as migrants is useful, politically progressive, and helps human beings. Sometimes, the opposite can be true as well. Sometimes, thinking of a place as home can also be politically progressive, and help human beings. And sometimes, it may just be the truth.

***

It is not surprising that Wendy Doniger expects us to accord greater value in our thoughts to a piece of rock's journey over 50 million years to become India rather than to our living memory of who we are and where we have been living for at least a few thousand years now. Given a long enough time span, even a rock can be proved to have come from somewhere else. But there is more than a settler/native dichotomy at work in this particular example. It reflects an even more subtle bias in thinking that affects how we narrate histories today, human, and 'natural' history too. It also affects deeply how historians see Hinduism, and is perhaps the single biggest difference in terms of how we see Hinduism and they fail to do so.

To understand this bias, we must understand first the idea of modernity. Modernity, in the social sciences, refers not just to being 'new', but the social, cultural, philosophical, political, and economic forms that arose around the world roughly in the past 500 years. It is modernity's cultural and philosophical biases that are relevant here (or we could say, its 'epistemology,' or, simply, a discussion about how we know what we know). We associate modernity with the triumph of reason and science. Colonial modernity, of course, told us that the triumph was specifically of Western reason over our Hindu superstition, of their science over our religion. Post-independence, we persisted in perpetuating this highly culturally specific denial of our own indigenous systems of knowledge, denigrating many of our beliefs as superstitions. We perhaps tried to compensate for this by also beginning to reimagine our ancient past as a newly independent modern nation would, asserting and celebrating our rediscovery of scientific prowess in ancient India. The issue here though is not with science or who had it first. It has to do with the way some biases in modern epistemology continue to distort reality, without our ever knowing it.

Consider how the story of the world is taught today. Picture the numerous illustrations we have seen in science books, children's books, and TV shows:

In the beginning was a Big Bang. Then hot gases swirled and settled into stars. Then bits of rock fell off and went hurling around in orbits. Then, the fires on earth cooled. Then, the chemical soup on earth somehow sparked, and then we had Life!

End, part one of story.

Let us examine this, not just for what it says, but how it says it. We don't have to refute it, nor are we 'Creationists' in that sense to argue with it. It is precisely because we agree with science's account of the world that we critique it, not because we are superstitious and disagree with it altogether.

What we notice in this particular way of narrating the history of the universe is the primacy of the physical over the biological. We speak of things, objects, fires, gases, and then finally, chemicals. Life, at best, we note as a matter of process, of chemistry.

This view, which arose with the rise of scientific method during modernity, is not inaccurate, and it is useful. In fact, it has been enormously successful in that it has allowed us to learn and control nature. But in the end, it only views everything as it does the parts of a machine. Our TV scientists may extol the wonders of science, but none of it can help ease the pain; we do not quite see life as life sees itself when we break it up in our knowledge into machine-parts. There is a name for this phenomenon, this bias which makes us de-animate reality, so to speak. It has been described as necrophilia[4], and it has been blamed, rightly in my view, for the vast destructiveness of modernity, its world wars and industrial strength environmental devastation, and hardening of human hearts into fears, anxieties, and abusiveness. It is a feature of modernity, of how we view the world and ourselves today. It is a part of commonsense. We look at everything as we would an object, a machine. We objectify women's bodies as pleasure-inducing parts. We pretend animals' screams at the slaughter house do not exist, or at best, they do not mean they are in pain. Our language itself reveals its bias. In English, we rarely say 'lives' in the Hindu sense of *'jeevi'* but only 'living *things*'. We watch terrible movies about torture and dismemberment and pursue body-mutilation as an art-form.

Then, as if to compensate for what we have forgotten, we have a pop culture infested with talking sponges, French-fries packets, cars, planes, and other objects cheerfully and literally animated.

All this distorts Hindu histories, and Hinduism too, profoundly.

> Hinduism is biocentric. It is life immersed in itself.

Consider this notable example. Richard Dawkins[5], a scientist-atheist in a long crusade against his peoples' religion now expanded to include *us* declares: in the beginning, we Hindus believe, a blue god sleeping on a fanged serpent ordered his servant to create the universe, and so he did.

This allegation about what we believe is presented alongside other colourful animal fantasy illustrations and allegations about how Mayans, Incans, Aboriginal Australians, and others believed the universe was created in their primitive ignorance long, long ago (and that is why now they are mostly extinct, for that; they didn't have the science to keep up, you see, only their religion, that seems to be the insinuation here).

It is another matter that no Hindu today takes something like that literally. We just think of Lord Vishnu as we would a father. We would think of Goddess Lakshmi as we would a mother. There is one important lesson to thinking of a fatherly or a motherly divinity as the creator. It helps us recognize that we are in life, and our origins cannot be removed from it.

In the beginning, for us, is a mother. Not a fossil, not a spirit. But the sensibility of a child's devotion for a mother. That is our creation story. Nothing more.

We are in awe of endless beginning. We are ever at the beginning of the endless.

How else could we be? How could we presume to be above the immensities of time and infinity?

The modern worldview cannot recognize the splendour of the devotional and poetic view of creation because it does not value the living. No matter how much the Sagans and Dysons try, there is only so much excitement one can drum up in a worldview that is always outside us, below us, as if it were, awaiting our gaze, scrutiny, discussion. It is the machine view of the modern mind. That is why at best it sees our gods too as primitive names for machine-forces.

Hinduism is biocentric. It is life immersed in itself. It does not presume to gaze over reality. It is not machinist, it is not speciesist, it is not anthropocentric[6].

***

The second part of the story of life that we grow up with today also stands at odds with the realities of Hinduism. This is the way the story of evolution is rendered in simple ideas, catch-phrases, and in pop culture (though Hindus have not had reason to see a conflict between the truth of evolution itself and their own cultural narratives). In this narrative, nature is depicted as little more than a place of ruthless, violent, competition for survival. Each species fights and kills each other, until someone wins. This is the most common way in which children learn about nature, and natural history today. Dominance and blood are the idioms by which we learn about life.

Scientific theories and popular culture myths about prehistory and the origins of mankind[7] tell us as much about our present as they do about the past. In the 1850s, for example, when Darwin's ideas entered the public consciousness, the impulse was to look at the stages of evolution in terms of inventiveness and tools, a typical idiom perhaps for the early industrial age. It was also not uncommon to apply a simplistic Darwinian notion of competition to the political realities of the day; placing European nations and races, for example, in a higher evolutionary level than say Africans and others. It was the age of social Darwinism and racism. It was easy to talk about the dominance and cruelty of some groups of people as but merely natural, just survival of the fittest, rather than as an aberration.

Even if we are more sensitive to the idea of social Darwinism today, the way we tell our stories about cavemen, hunter-gatherers, monkeys, apes, dinosaurs, evolution, and all of life before what we call history, remains highly biased[8]. The only thing that dominates the picture we have of millions of years of natural history is killing. Animated dinosaur films, exciting National Geographic wildlife documentaries, story-books, games, every story our culture tells today about nature, wildlife, and prehistoric life is constructed around hunting, mauling, killing, eating. Occasionally, the stories break for mating; but usually after depicting a suitably bloody fight between suitors first.

We consume all this, and we often say, *that's nature*.

But really, it isn't. This is an especially narrow, selective, culturally specific view of nature. Compare Hindu, Buddhist and Jain folk tales about animals for example, with modern hunt and kill narratives. We may laugh at our animal stories and consider them kids' stuff because the animals talk. But we do not realize that in our culture we recognize the sanctity of non-human life, and we see the similarities between motherhood, friendship, kindness, love, in birds and animals as much as we do in human life too. Our civilization didn't suddenly get this quirk late in the day after being exposed to other civilizations that believed animals were either machines or just resources put here for our consumption. It is Hinduism's understanding of nature, and it is important to acknowledge this difference.

In today's mass mediated civilization though, with its pop science, and pop Darwinism, we see animal life much like we would an entertainment, a particularly bloody videogame. Animals are seen like machine parts; hunting machines, mating machines, competing machines, surviving machines, killing machines, eating machines. It is sort of like how modern industrial civilization views human beings too, that much is true; a mixture of anthropocentrism, necrophilia, social functionalism, and a simplified Darwinism[9].

> **The view of nature, natural history, and human pre-history that we have today is highly distorted.**

But in any case, what we need to recognize first is this. The view of nature, natural history, and human pre-history that we have today is highly distorted. It is perhaps inevitable then that Hinduism's most ancient and cherished scriptures are also misinterpreted, egregiously.

***

The contents of a child's history textbook from India, seen one day, in a California hospital waiting room, out of all places:

Adi-manav, primitive man, scratching lines in caves and hunting game; Indus Valley; Aryans. Civilization. Cities.

We think of civilization as an ascent out of nature into construction; citadels and great baths and roads and drainage; chariots and wheels and spears and swords.

We think of nature as savage and primitive, mating and killing, no more.

If we lose these two myths, the history of humanity, and not just Hinduism, will look very different from what it does now.

***

Hinduphobia is essentially the anti-Hindu front of nothing less than an ideology of violence.

CHAPTER 4

THE MYTH OF VEDIC VIOLENCE

Words of praise for God are not about mutilation

No word has been abused more in modern histories of Hinduism than the Vedas, and no word in its universe more abused perhaps than 'sacrifice'.

What is this sacrifice a philologist plunders our heritage for? What is this blood-lust? What lies really in our Great Mother Sanskrit that the dungeon-keepers of dead dictionaries will not readily admit to? The chief claim of the Hinduphobic theorists is this:

The Vedas were words that were chanted when animals (and sometimes humans) were being killed.

There is also a corollary claim now from this school of theorizing: the Vedas were also about killing and eating cows[1].

Modern assertions of history, from Left and from Right, take liberties with identities and presumptions. The arguments are over totalities, whether ancient Hindus ate beef or not, whether they were violent or not. The truth may be simple: all of the people who lived at that time may not have been this way or that way; but the *sensibilities* of Hindu thought cannot be reduced so conveniently to insist that this is how Hinduism arose, in violence, human-sacrifice, and cattle-sacrifice, until the kind Mughal emperor put an end to it centuries later. We need not shy away from the question of violence. Did people in ancient India kill? Quite possibly, for it is difficult to imagine a time or place without some kind of violence. But was killing a way of life, or even central to a way of life, in ancient India? And more important, was killing sanctioned as *a central idea* in Hindu philosophy in ancient times, or even in later times?

We know the answer in our hearts, in our minds, and in our lives.

Think of what you feel when someone outside of Hinduphobic discourse mentions the Vedas. Say, your grandmother. Or a spiritual figure you admire, say Swami Vivekananda, or even a renunciant at your local temple speaking in your language. Think of the gods and goddesses who appear in your mind, and think of the words of praise and surrender you associate with them. You might think of *Aditi*, and *Savitri*, and *Agni*, and *Varuna*, and *Vayu*. You might think of the effect those words have on you, on your breath, your heart, your consciousness, your idea about the world even. You might think, perhaps, of God, and no other.

Now, think of the 'Vedas' in Hinduphobic history. Doniger, for example, begins her chapter on "Humans, Animals and Gods in the Rig Veda" by declaring her intent to confront violence in the Vedas and show how their alleged ritual violence supports some alleged social violence[2]. In a less gory form, we also encountered the Hinduphobic idea of the Vedas in some of our own modern history textbooks. In school, in our history exam, the right answer to a question about the Vedas might have said little more than that they were hymns and rituals about nature. The condescension may not have been direct, but it was implicit. For something our spiritual leaders and cultural reformers have invoked repeatedly as our intellectual source, so to speak, if not the mystical origin itself, we were amazingly indifferent in our education towards the Vedas.

Today, as modern Hindus become more interested in the discourse about who we are, and what our thought really meant, we realize the gap, and don't quite know how to address it yet.

Compare an Indian publisher's book on the Vedas with an international academic book. You will be fortunate to find even a little in common. In one, you will see what you know as gods. You will see devotion, and poetry. In the other, you will see a sterility that says more about the echo chambers of academe in which they were made for the last two centuries, than about the Vedas perhaps.

Inaccuracies, distortions, and even unsubstantiated whims on the part of Hinduphobic scholarship have been pointed out, even if in the popular corners of the internet (and in some academic responses too)[3]. However, in this chapter, we go beyond arguments about the meaning of words, translations, and interpretations. In my view, the source of the Hinduphobic distortion of the Vedas as texts of violence is not simply from a mere lack of understanding of Hinduism, but from a *deeper lack of self-reflexivity about the mythology of violence in Western thought itself*. There are some ground assumptions about nature and violence in Western social thought, and even more so in today's pop culture, that make some beliefs, theories and stories seem only 'natural' to everyone today (including non-Westerners as well, thanks to media and globalization). One reason Hinduphobic scholarship sees so much violence in Hinduism where we do not is perhaps because its intellectual toolbox is yet to evolve a suitable critique of violence itself[4]. Opponents of Hinduphobia too often fall short on this count. We can recognize the problems with the often preposterous sexualization of our sacred meanings by Hinduphobic interpreters, but we often do not recognize just how much more problematic their imputation of violence to our thought might be as well.

Hinduphobia is essentially the anti-Hindu front of nothing less than an ideology of violence. It is not merely a religious or racial rivalry between them and us. It is profound existential error on their part. They fail to see the cultural specificity of their own beliefs about violence, and worse, presume universality based upon their own past practices of violence, perhaps, and it is that failure that we will have to address, for the sake of all[5].

***

Let us begin with an example, with what they say about our alleged human sacrificing, beef-eating Vedic ancestors.

According to current scholarship, the Vedic Aryans (our alleged forefathers) brought along on their horses to the Punjab a *culture of sacrifice* as a form of 'insurance'.

As Doniger puts it, the culture of sacrifice is all about fear that without sacrifice, the sun wouldn't rise the next day[6].

This supposed fear about the sun not rising might sound familiar, though not from the experience of ever having listened to the Vedas being chanted. You and I may be excused therefore for not being aware of this Vedic *sloka* that orders sacrifice to get the sun to rise tomorrow. You and I may only have known the Vedas as hymns of adoration for the divine.

Yet, you and I, according to the historians who define our world, belong to a lineage of exactly that kind of violent superstition.

The Hindoos must do Veda sacrifice now, or the sun won't rise!

Perhaps this sounds familiar. It should. You have surely encountered it before. The caricatured Incas in a Tintin comic said that, a Belgian fantasy of sun-worshipping Indians, of another kind. The perforated and relentlessly cruel Aztecs in the movie *Apocalypto* might have thought that too; an Australo-Hollywood liberal-backlash fantasy[7].

Every stereotype of the 'other', the non-European, repeats this myth; that the natives believed that without sacrifice, without violence and bloodshed, nature would not behave, that the sun would not rise.

It fits well with the story of world history, of progress, concocted in the colonial era and allowed to spread across the planet into mini-national fantasies in the postcolonial one:

Once upon a time, the world was primitive, superstitious and violent.

Then, thanks to Greece and Christianity, Europe had Enlightenment and Science.

Now, thanks to Europe and Science, the whole world is almost developed and out of its benighted past.

***

But consider this.

Why would anyone in the tropics fear that the sun would not rise?

Why would Hindus or Incas, Aztecs or Mayans, or anyone in this belt of latitudes have that kind of a doubt?

Or is it just an ice-age far-north paranoia about long winters and longer nights? Perhaps, maybe, the source of all this is the weather....

***

The Hinduism expert tells us something about our weather too. According to Doniger, the monsoon's "violence" and "uncertainty" create a perennial psychological condition in us that gives us our beliefs about our whimsical and violent gods[8].

This is not a pop theory from the 19th century colonial fantasy to explain tropical tribal superstition. This is the present. This is the cutting-edge of leading Hinduism expertise.

Let us begin with this view of the monsoon. For us, the monsoon is not a deadly storm like an itch in jealous Zeus's beard. To anyone who knows India, or the Hindus, really knows us, that is; for someone who comes to us and opens their eyes and ears and listens and watches, and gets off their own solitary mind-fantasy, the monsoon is not about violence, but merely a blessing and a festival.

Think of Kalidasa. Read the classics. Watch *Lagaan*. Watch a thousand Bollywood movies. The Indian mind does not associate the monsoon with violence.

The only meaning we have for the monsoon is that it marks the return of everything to life. It is relief from the heat. It is children laughing, peacocks dancing, the sound of frogs, plants growing, life renewed, hope. And our gods too are like our monsoon. They give us life. We welcome their return, again and again.

We do not think of our gods as capricious.

Our god stories are totally about causality, *karma*, reason. No one is whimsical; even Narada, we tell ourselves, is only seemingly an itinerant troublemaker. He sets things in motion that will lead to ultimate good.

Our stories do not tell us our gods are irrationally violent. Forceful, yes, but not without reason. Our sensibility does not teach us to fear them as much as to trust them, worship them, and believe in their fairness; even when we sometimes complain. A devotional view of the divine does not come from a position of uncertainty and fear.

It appears to be a foreign thing.

Maybe... it's *their* weather.

***

There is perhaps a deeper, older meteorological explanation for Eurocentrism too.

The Ice-Age. Then the long cold icy winters of the far North.

Let us therefore picture the following scenario of ice-age reasoning, Bugs Bunny and Elmer Fudd cartoon style:

One still dark morning, long ago, in a bleak village somewhere in the snow, a little bald-headed man goes a-hunting. His name is Ugh.

Me, Ugh! Brave hunter!

Maybe, he is singing too.

A-hunting in the snow, a-hunting in the snow...

Suddenly, he spies a rabbit.

Unlike his cartoon descendant who never manages to get his 'wabbit' prey, though, Ugh is lucky.

He stabs the rabbit with his flint-chip spear. He kills it, literally.

And just then, the sun rises, and an epiphany takes place:

Ugh spill rabbit-blood.

Rabbit-blood look like sun.

Ugh make sun rise!

Fanfare! Drumroll! *2001: A Space Odyssey* moment.

Cue *Also Sprach Zarathustra*.

***

Though historians are yet to honestly explore this question as far as I know, the obsession with meteorological uncertainty and violence in general might actually well turn out to be a long-standing symptom of ice-age survival instincts and beliefs. While the current biases of academia (except against Hinduism that is) have been named accurately as Eurocentrism and such by the Left (while upset Hindus inaccurately go after 'deserts'), there is perhaps a deeper, older meteorological explanation for Eurocentrism too: the Northern European climate, especially its once harshly chilly prehistoric conditions.

Faced with bleak, lifeless landscapes of deadly ice, the primitive hunters of the once-distant European North developed a hardy, physical, violent attitude to nature and to life. It permeated their behaviour, belief, and mythology for centuries. Despite some notable encounters with non-ice age conditions and cultures in later years, some of these ice-age superstitions were difficult to dislodge. For example they did not believe until their encounter with India in the 1600s that one could survive completely on a plant-based diet[9]. Their diet was understandable given their habitat, but what was more problematic on the whole for the rest of the world was their disbelief about the realities of the rest of the world. They were for a very long time on the whole not very empathetic. But they were ambitious and turned the whole world into a mini-ice-age mental factory, normalizing ice-age views of diet, life, and survival all over the world[10].

One explanation for the stubborn ethnocentrism of their worldview, we must now consider, is the fact these primitive hunters were often the only ones looking out god-like at vast expanses of snow-covered land and ice. Unlike the warm tropics, where every life-form knew its place from birth as a part of a gigantic, living, universe of insects, birds, plants, animals, and people, the ice-age hunters perhaps felt righteously alone and understandably superior in all of existence.

And when, occasionally, another life-form raised its small and unfortunate head, they usually killed it and ate it.

They were survivors. Their original way of life was survivalism. Centuries later, when their descendants took on new names, faiths, and lands, they took that survivalism with them; to the Americas, to the tropics, and in time, enshrined it into every theory of science and history they could. That might be one reason, yet to be discovered, why current theories of science and history seem to be enamoured so much by theories about violence and sacrifice, and about the weather too.

***

For someone illustrated here with a comical example though, Ugh has left a powerful legacy in the world. His mind is still here, having lasted through the ice-age, dark-age, and the enlightened-age. The shadow of his thought and prejudice run down the halls of centuries of education, knowledge, commonsense, and in lands far away from ice-age desperation too.

Ugh comes to a Vishnu temple in sunny Kishkindha and calls the Garuda Ratha "that thing ... for human sacrifice," like the Juggernaut! That pagan devil-God machines that the Brachmanes drove, crushing superstitious natives under their wheels!

Ugh comes to the world of our Gods and sees his own unfortunate past, devils in his mind, demons in his actions.

Ugh sees our celebration of nature, our equal regard for animals, and deems it primitive animal worship, or a fear of reincarnation.

Ugh puts on his academic mask and chews on the words of the *Purusha Sukta*, hallucinating a horrid ritual of cutting, chopping and dismemberment (when Ugh got a modern religion, by his standards, they learned to regulate the violence and call it 'sacrifice', you lose some, you get some).

***

Frankly, only massively egocentric cultures would believe that without sacrifice, the sun would not rise the next day.

Not the Hindus.

Not the ones who chant a Gayatri Mantra.

Not the ones who wake before dawn, when stars are still visible, and chant, *We Adore* to the rising sun.

Why would Hindus, or humans, or any living being accustomed to rising, accustomed to witnessing the whole of life rising, with the sun, each morning, ever presume to fear that the sun wouldn't rise tomorrow?

> By presuming savagery as the default condition, historians are ever ready to prove that early Vedic Hinduism was violent too.

Why would Hindus, who see the Divine in the smallest of creatures, presume to control the center of this whole visible firmament itself through superstitions of sacrifice?

Yet, the experts on Hinduism say this is who we are; a superstitious bloodthirsty lot. And debating this claim makes you a Hindu fundamentalist.

On that note, the *Purusha Sukta*, according to current scholarship, is about cutting and chopping some poor man too, and also the foundation for the caste-system.

I first heard it being chanted in the presence of a lower-caste child of an Indian village that millions came to adore as an *avatar* of god. I heard it chanted seated on the floor crammed into thousands of devotees of too many nationalities and castes for anyone to miss the point about what the poem seemed to saying; perceive all of these hands, eyes, feet not as those of thousands of different individuals, but simply as manifestations of the divine One.

***

There are two reasons for the persistence of the myth of Vedic violence. At one level, it is geopolitical. It is the old colonizer's myth about the superstitious natives, steeped in brutality and in need of civilizing forces, such as either a colonial religion or secular rule of law. Since Eurocentrism and colonialism are nominally over, there is something else that obviously persists. At a deeper level, the myth of Vedic violence is connected to an unexamined ethnocentric presumption about the normativity of violence. The belief that human nature, and nature, generally are innately and relentlessly

The Myth of Vedic Violence

violent in the same manner as the violence of our times, of our world wars and industrialized slaughter as a way of life era, is the deepest and most harmful myth of the modern world[11].

By presuming violence to be the default state of nature with which natural history, and human history, all begin, Hinduphobic historians perpetuate both a deep rooted normativity about the place of violence in nature, and more specifically, Hinduphobic denial of our cultural realities as well. Naturally, the verses of the Vedas, which, for the most part we see as words of adoration, words of praise for the divine, can appear to them to be only grunts and curses to accompany dismemberment of the Ugh-Make-Meat-Pie-in-Man-Cave fantasy.

We have challenged these claims, but we need to go further. We need to flesh out a crucial missing link in the history of Hinduism.

How does the religion of allegedly primitive, prehistoric, brutal, savage, bloodthirsty grunting killers (which is what today's commonsense and popular culture tell us prehistoric humans were, and Hinduphobic historians tell us Vedic Hindus in particular were) become a religion of ideals like *ahimsa, samskara, sabhyata, dharma*?

At one level, the problem may well lie in the popular view today of the conduct of our prehuman ancestors, and the animal world in general. By presuming savagery as the default condition, historians are ever ready to prove that early Vedic Hinduism was violent too, and it is only much later that the present day sensibilities associated with Hinduism like devotion and non-violence arise. The implication, of course, is that this was due to the civilizing influences hailing down on the subcontinent from the West (Western Asia with its egalitarian religions and Western Europe with its scientific acumen).

However.

What if the past was not what it has been presumed to be?

> We say it's all survival of the fittest, though what we are witnessing really is better described as the propaganda of the cruellest.

Let us examine the unstated assumptions about history and prehistory. Even if the Vedas, the usual 'starting point' for Hindu history, were composed only a couple of thousand years ago, what existed before? Were the people who lived before what we consider the beginning of history merely hunters and killers?

It seems very unlikely. If you have seen monkeys, birds, elephants, virtually most animals, if you have known them on the terms of reality and not through wildlife TV show narratives, you know their nature. They can be violent, some more than others, according their dictates of hunger. But then, beyond that, they are not besotted by bloodshed in the way modern man is. They are not living bloodshed as a way of life, thought, and culture[12].

Most humans probably were just like that once.

Except perhaps those forced into exceptional levels of violence by exceptional conditions.

Violence is the foundational mythology of what was once Western, and what has become now, global modern thought. It is the last barrier, the one border of imagination that even the most critical intellects rarely manage to cross. Today's academy has successfully challenged many of its recent prejudices and superstitions about identity, about sexism and racism, for instance. But it does not make room for Hindus, as we have seen. One reason for this is that making room for Hinduism, a genuine room, beyond tokenism, would mean opening the door to questions about its own ethical and intellectual bottom-line; and that is its naturalization of violence.

We can look at the problem this way. Today, a modern education in any school or college provides the tools to recognize sexism and racism. But does it provide the tools to look at this world and notice its violence? Does it equip a student to name cruelty? On the contrary, it teaches us, for example, that it is perfectly acceptable for millions of mice, frogs, and other small creatures to be cut up and killed by thousands of reluctant school children around the world each day.

We do not cut up the earth to show what's inside. We do not cut up anything else.

Why only animals? Why will an illustration not suffice?

What vivisection is really teaching us is not biology but an ideology; call it speciesism, necrophilia, scientism, Darwinist fatalism. In the end, it teaches millions of children that the *suffering of a living being is inconsequential*. It teaches them to harden their hearts, dehumanize themselves, and unnaturalize themselves, all in the great cause of science.

***

The world today does not name violence as violence. Instead, it calls it nature. This is one of the most pervasive, deeply held beliefs in the world today, reinforced tightly between the modern school curriculum and pop culture.

We watch a children's documentary on insects. It goes through the usual narrative of birth, growth, competition, and mating. Then, suddenly, it culminates with a butterfly being devoured by another creature, shards of wing floating around the hall in 3D slow motion. We watch it, a bit uncomfortable. But lacking the intellectual resources in a society that suppresses our natural ability to respond to it as we should, we only say, 'that's nature', we only say 'circle of life', as the pop philosopher puts it in the voiceover.

At best, we call it an inappropriate creative choice for a children's film.

We don't call it a particular cultural, historical, ethnic view of nature, though that is exactly what it is.

We watch a wildlife documentary of cheetahs chasing and killing and eating a deer. We forget that possibly happens once a day. For the most part animals do not go around fighting and killing. They are playing, resting, exchanging affections with their own not unlike how we do. Our natural intelligence may recognize that, and lead us to describe them in simple human terms like mothers and children, brothers and sisters, not unlike the ways in which folk tales talk about animal characters.

But the exalted scientific narrative presses itself again. The narrator refers to the animals in the show not as living beings, but as political players; the 'dominant male', the 'alpha', and so on. Dominance might exist in nature, and so does violence. But it is a human, and a cultural choice to focus on these and ignore the rest. It makes a specific social group's political choice to dominate others and to use killing as a way of life seem very natural.

As human beings, as living beings, we know nature, still. But as the products of an exceptionally cruel phase in human history and thought, we lack the cultural permission to act appropriately. We go to zoos and not knowing what to do before unaccustomed forms of life's presence, get awkward and taunt and tease the animals. Even when we don't, we only see the narrative that today's science gives us, the narrative of dominance and hierarchies.

We only see dominance. We only recognize violence. That is what our culture teaches us to do. We say it's all survival of the fittest, though what we are witnessing really is better described as the propaganda of the cruelest.

From Darwinian survivalism to the naturalization of violence is a small step. If we extend our scope now to violence in the media and pop culture, if we look at the story that all our movies, TV shows, videogames, books, and comics are putting out about violence, we

> Knowing pain, and knowing that it is not a good thing, is one of the most elemental forms of nature's intelligence.

can see how pervasive and widespread the naturalization of violence is today. It is no longer one of many elements in the media, but almost the entirety of the media environment itself[13].

Think of movies like *Natural Born Killers, Fight Club, Saw, Hostel*, and TV shows like *Game of Thrones*, and most of all the so-called Reality Shows like *Survivor*. Think even of literary classics like *Lord of the Flies*.

These stories do not simply feature violence because it is fun. They are hammering home a deeper message about the naturalness and the inevitability of violence. Without rules, *Lord of the Flies* says, children become violent savages, it's *nature*. Without pretence, adults will turn into scheming, nasty, selfish 'survivors', a TV genre says, it's *reality*.

Generations of media audiences have grown up believing that human nature is savage, cruel, and violent. We rarely stop to think if savagery and cruelty are really natural or merely effects of specific historical, political, economic, or cultural conditions.

The movie *Fight Club* asks, for instance, how much do you know of yourself unless you are in a fight?

Hinduism has dealt with violence long enough to know you do not need to be in a fight to know it is bad.

The movie *Fight Club* has a memorable line, on the same point: you are not the kind of clothes you wear or the work you do.

You are you when you are in a fight. It's real.

Violence is a certain sort of culture's indicator of authenticity.

Ours is the opposite. We believe that without *Ahimsa*, *Satya* is impossible, and that without *Satya*, *Ahimsa* is impossible. Truth and Non-violence are inseparable. We cannot understand truth if we are not non-violent in thought, word, and deed. We cannot be non-violent if we are not respectful of truth.

The word 'Hin-du', it is said, is derived from *'Himsa'* and *'Duramu'*: one who stays far from cruelty; an unusual, if inspiring saying[14].

Our epics have battles. Sure. The gods have weapons. Sure. But the philosophy of the epics is exactly about the dilemma of violence; about the human yearning to govern it, minimize its use. There is no denial of the consequence of violence in our stories. There is no pornography around pain in our stories.

There is no superstition around killing in our stories.

Violence has consequences. Everything has consequences. That is the heart of Hindu sensibility, whether we want to call it *karma* or *dharma*, determinism or agency, what we are given and what we do with it, history or freedom from it.

We do not view violence as a tool to ensure either authenticity or meaning. But what we confront today is the complete opposite. Histories of Hinduism that fantasize about violence reveal not only the usual biases such as Eurocentrism and Orientalism, but a deep-rooted obsession with violence that is very peculiar to its own history, and that of few others. This is not to say others have no violence in their history. It is just that the Western academy, which today is

---

> They have been passed on and they have survived, simply because the intelligence in our stories still speaks to us.

more or less the global academy, is ruled by certain beliefs about the naturalness of violence more deeply than it perhaps realizes.

***

Consider some of the sayings in the English language:

Dog Eat Dog.

Big Fish eat Small Fish.

Eat or be eaten.

Kill or be killed.

Today's commonsense sayings and beliefs are not innocent and innocuous. They belong to a worldview specific to one of the most violent encounters in global history. Colonialism was not simply about land-grabbing, not simply about religious coercion, or about the plunder of nature and labour. It was at its rawest about the establishment of violence as the unquestioned ground of all further human endeavour. Colonialism might have bequeathed to us a seemingly civilized code of regulation afterwards, rules and laws, rights and justice. But what it has done to culture, to humanity's capacity for feeling the pain of others who live is nearly irreparable. Knowing pain, and knowing that it is not a good thing, is one of the most elemental forms of nature's intelligence, and under modernity, we have nearly lost it.

We live now in a world where violence and dominance is seen as the norm, as nature, even if we have more rules and laws to regulate it. Even Mahatma Gandhi began his life believing in the propaganda of violence, presuming himself to be weak and lacking somehow, experimenting with the superior powers' supposedly superior diet which supposedly gave them their strengths. The verse Gandhi heard often during his childhood[15]:

"Behold the mighty Englishman.
He rules the Indian small,

And Hinduphobic history claiming to love Hinduism is like a scientist writing a book on cooking with insects in order to encourage children to take an interest in insect life (or death, actually).

Because being a meat-eater
He is five cubits tall."
Beefeaters rule Muttoneaters.
Muttoneaters rule Planteaters.

Europe over West Asia; West Asia over South Asia; Europe over World!

The larger your violence-footprint, the superior you are. The larger your appetite, literally, the greater your glory. During colonialism, diet, Darwin, and racism all came together[16] conveniently in the colonizer's fantasy. We may have learned to challenge parts of this equation today, but not quite all of it yet.

Decolonization still has a long way to go.

***

The naturalization of predation, especially in the political context of human affairs, is very different from merely acknowledging that predators exist in nature. Look at any book about dinosaurs, animals, wildlife. Watch any wildlife show on TV. The story is told almost always around the hunt, and the act of killing, bloodshed, and dismemberment. A story is a creative selection. There are other ways of telling stories about nature. Yet, our dominant story structure is predicated on killing.

That's a hunter-gatherer's view of nature. Not a Hindu one. Not a view of anyone grounded in the reality of the enormity of violence and killing, small or big.

In our stories, animals and birds speak, feel, appeal to divinity and to humanity's respect for ethical propriety.

Our modern Hindu minds must now relearn how to recognize something profoundly significant in the existence of these stories: they are a recognition of the right of animals, the right of life to exist. It is only our anthropocentrism that insists the animals in our stories must be code for outcasts and subalterns. Sometimes, an elephant is just a Ganesha.

If it weren't for the modern animal rights movement, the world today would probably still be teaching its young the 'scientific' truth that animals don't feel pain.

***

Hindu sensibility might understand this. An intelligent sensibility, whether it calls itself Hindu, or not, might also understand this. These are issues of value, meaning, and most of all, of ethics. These have been preserved and passed down for many generations now, mother to child, father to child, in love, kindness, play, laughter, wit, happiness, and insightfulness. These have been passed on not through doctrine or dogma or propaganda. They have been passed on and they have survived, simply because the intelligence in our stories still speaks to us.

Hinduism is sensibility renewing itself again and again.

It is not like a theory of life taught in classrooms today, to memorize and regurgitate, names, parts, functions, and no grasp at all of the life itself in the whole; it is not what may be called the *techne* view of life; with animal lives broken up into stories of fights and copulations and murders; it is not the view of the vivisector that teaches us to ignore vast suffering, to foolishly and arrogantly say a sight of some organs just as well obtained from a book is somehow worth that pain.

It is a sensibility that comes from life being in life.

I believe there is a word for it, when life perceives life fully, from within, not as object, outside itself. It appears in the Gayatri Mantra. It is not unlike the feeling all of the living world feels at witnessing the first rays of the dawn. I like to translate it as:

I exult in adoring You.

***

A history of Hinduism is a history of life, of the truly deep meanings invested for thousands of years by a culture in a sense of sanctity for life.

It is not a history of social groups. It is not a history of their struggles for dominance. It is not a history of their weapons or their gadgets. It is not a history of their magical powers. It is not a history of insanity and violence.

It is a history of love, of humanity's yearning to find love, in life, in this world, and most of all, in impossible situations.

It is a history of surviving the fallibility of human action, of confronting inhumanity in times that are profoundly dehumanizing; about kingdoms (or just homes) being grabbed by greedy family members, about exiles, separations, heartbreaks, and still, about being able to live. And live with the least amount of harm in return. It is about finding strength, without deploying that strength as domination, as a denial of the dignity of the other.

Hinduphobic history does not see any of this, not one bit of it.

Hinduphobic history likes to pretend the Hindus are sitting in sarcophagi under eons of sand and dust, awaiting their discoverer's benevolent gaze.

Hinduphobic history is like pinning butterflies to a board to witness their beauty.

Hinduphobic history is like slashing open salmon trapped by a dam to scoop out their eggs and squeezing milt from the male salmon into them.

> I believe there is a word for it, when life perceives life fully, from within, not as object, outside itself. It appears in the Gayatri Mantra. It is not unlike the feeling all of the living world feels at witnessing the first rays of the dawn. I like to translate it as: "I exult in adoring You."

And Hinduphobic history claiming to love Hinduism is like a scientist writing a book on cooking with insects in order to encourage children to take an interest in insect life (or death, actually).

This, too, is a real example[17].

***

But in our hearts, we cannot ever think of the deeds of our gods as mere fairy-tales.

Chapter 5

THE MYTH OF A HINDU HISTORY WITHOUT A HINDU VIEW OF GOD

Rejecting the epistemic premise and narrative arc of Hinduphobic history

The Hinduphobic historians' view of Hinduism likes to put its demons before our gods. A Hindu view of the divine, a sense of how we feel, know, and speak about God, is perhaps the single greatest absence in their stories. This is not to say only a Hindu knows his God and others don't, or that only a Hindu can speak about Hinduism. No. We typically don't have issues about ownership. But we do have a limit to tolerance when it comes to inaccuracy. When a certain line in logic, truth, and of course propriety in the face of a community's sense of the sacred are systematically violated, we have to raise the obvious question:

Can you speak of a history of 'the Christians', or 'the Jews', or 'the Muslims', without some mention of what God means to the people who profess these faiths?

You could have a history of a people, a tribe, a race, a nationality, perhaps without having to speak of their views of the divine. If your definition is based on geography, or some kind of demographic criterion, then such an absence would not be relevant. But a history of *The Hindus*, a group defined essentially on the basis of a shared sense of religiosity, would be meaningless if we ignored how the members of this group share at least some cultural and philosophical sensibilities around their understanding of the sacred. It is doubly important in Hindu culture, for all the obvious reasons; we do not have a sense of ourselves as a Hindu people, traditionally speaking; our common-name, so to speak, was itself given to us by foreigners, a loose geographical appellation grown now to represent nearly a whole one-fifth of humanity; and most of all, the intellectual assault on our integrity, the argument that we are not a religion or a people at all, just a right-wing fundamentalist fantasy.

Our sense of ourselves as being Hindu may be a historically recent phenomenon, and not unrelated to the politics of colonialism and the postcolonial legacies of nationalism and partition. But our sense of Hinduism, our understanding of God, and our lives in relation to God, are all far older than current scholarship acknowledges, and at the very least not unimportant to any credible academic account of our history. Contrary to most academic accounts that give such an appearance, for us Hinduism is not primarily about the caste-system. It is about our gods and goddesses; our child-gods, and our mother-goddesses, our animal gods, and our literally innumerable gurus, local deities, *avatars*, and other sacred figures.

Our view of life, our practice of life, our history, our politics, our successes and failures, our striving for ethical ideals, our occasional lapses, all of our world is connected somehow to this.

Yet, a really big book called *The Hindus* has very little to say about how we Hindus view the divine, accurately at least.

***

This is a widespread problem in Hinduphobic historiography.

We have identified some of the cultural sources of this problem; modernity's anthropocentrism, necrophilia, speciesism, selective Darwinism, and the more apparent biases of Eurocentrism. We have seen how these demons, so to speak, distort the official historian's view of Hinduism's past. It conforms to their own preconceived idea that nature is savagely violent, and so, naturally, our Vedic ancestors too. But all of this is only the beginning. It is set up fundamentally so as to bend the narrative of the rest of Hindu history too, to make it seem like what they think it is rather than what it really is. This simply is the official story of how Hinduism 'progresses' in their view:

In the beginning, Hinduism was nothing more than primitive superstitious nature worship; those Vedic cowboys saw fire and called it *Agni*! They feared lighting and called it *Indra*! Fearful of things they did not understand, lacking mathematics, foresight, scientific acumen, and a weather app, perhaps, they sought to control what we know now to be just simple natural phenomena through quaint customs like Vedic chanting and human sacrifice.

Then, centuries passed. The Hindus got some complexity in their heads, thanks to their encounter with various social groups as they wandered down past the Punjab. But most importantly, it was the civilizing influences from outside that made Hinduism what it is, or at least what its supporters say it is now.

The violent Vedic Hindus learned *ahimsa* thanks to the Buddha's rebellion against it.

The patriarchal Hindus learned women could be strong like Draupadi because of the Greek invasion that brought exposure to highly empowered Western feminism.

They try to break up the internal coherence of Hindu thought through a series of funny steps.

The Mughals, finally, regulated cow slaughter though even the Vedas called for beef curries; and now today the Hindus blame them — the nerve!

Then, once India got independence, the most common trope about India by the foreign press (or India-watchers, as our press used to call them): *will India survive?*

And then, most recently, the new trope: *will India turn Hindu-fascist?*

There is something about Hindus that seems to make others think they need to civilize us.

***

After insisting that Hinduism begins with the violence of invading Central Asians into India, the dominant historians now try to eviscerate from its philosophy its most essential precept: that God is one. Instead of acknowledging the common, persistent Hindu sensibility of seeing God as one, but also known through many names and forms, they try to break up the internal coherence of Hindu thought through a series of funny steps. In what might be better described as the 'first denial', rather than the 'first alliance', we are told by Doniger that the Vedas are pretty much stories of social oppression coded as gods and ogres. The feeling of devotion, which is what we associated with sacred stories, presumably does not come till the 'third alliance', centuries later. We have to wonder then if the people who chanted the same words that inspire devotion in us now felt something radically different simply because the expert says so. Or perhaps this is once again the civilizing fantasy at work; if Hinduism, like any religion at its best, seems to be about love, then it must be a recent development, a gift of redemption from more advanced civilizations.

Denial in place, Doniger proceeds with a rather convenient process of randomization on the Vedas. The early Vedic pantheon, we are told, was full of gods of varying importance, just like the pig characters from George Orwell's *Animal Farm*[1]. But somehow, these were only a collection of random supernatural beings, lacking the philosophical insight connecting them all together under the idea of one divinity, known through many forms, that would come much later. Just in case we thought that at the heart of Hinduism is this notion of one and many, Doniger writes that we see in the Rig Veda is a sort-of polytheism, with only the seeds of what will become monism in the Upanishadic age. Underneath a veil of vagueness masquerading as open-minded inquiry and exploration, there is just one Hinduphobic dogmatic assertion: a denial of the very core insight of Hindu thought that holds that God can be one and many.

This denial is a persistent tendency in Hinduphobic historiography. We may understand the Vedas and Upanishads as one coherent entity, even using words like Vedopanishad to describe them. Yet, Hinduphobic histories tell us that the Vedas and Upanishads mark very different stages of evolutionary development. They presume that the Vedas were a set of random wild stories about random wild supernatural beings being utterly and fantastically nasty to each other. It is only later, when Greek philosophy wakes up, and Gautama Buddha breaks up the Vedic age (according to them, that is), that we see the glimmer of those aspects of Hinduism that even Hinduphobic historians have not managed to distort and slander as of now.

After creating this artificial distinction between the supposedly violent and polytheistic Vedic age and the more contemplative and philosophical Upanishadic period, historians than go on to try and reduce the life of Hinduism that follows into what can only be described as a postmodernist paean to chaos. The epics, Doniger tells us, were probably just tall tales told by charioteers to soldiers between battles (note the perpetuation of the violence and war myth)[2]. It may be the case that the image we carry in our minds about Valmiki and Vyasa are somewhat mythic. What we imagine about the recitation of our sacred narratives, after all, are gentle

> We live in a world in which indifference to the suffering of others is an existential condition. It helps to think our gods and saints knew how to feel pain for others.

rishis in forest hermitages so pure and peaceful that even deer stand by attentively and listen. We do not know the literal truth of what it might have been. But we cannot take it for granted that smearing a story with blood and mud makes it any less mythic or any more 'real', except perhaps on reality TV shows and movies like *Saw* that is. If the idyllic hermitage was our popular cultural code once, the battlefield (and Ugh's cave) seems to the new code in academics and a certain fringe of pop culture to bestow authenticity to the past. It's real if it looks dirty. This *faux* reality-drive of course leads scholars to make learned-sounding declarations like how charioteers used to advise warriors. Perhaps they cannot see *Krishna* and *Arjuna* as *Krishna* and *Arjuna*, simply, as we do; *guru* and *shishya*, cousins in friendship, *avatar* and man.

For us, *Krishna* is *Krishna*.

***

As for *Rama*, who, for us, is *Rama*:

We are told that the 'tension' between *Rama*, *Sita* and *Lakshmana*, *that* kind of tension, that is, is a 'major motivation' in the Ramayana's story[3].

A dictionary defines 'perversion' as a 'distortion from an original meaning'. There is also *that* kind of sense in which 'perversion' is used. It may not be appropriate for one academic to use it to describe another academic's professional interpretation. The American Academy of Religions, in fact, has proclaimed the right of an academic to make *any* interpretation. So 'perversion' in *that* sense may be an inappropriate accusation to make and we shall not make it. But 'distortion from meaning' is perhaps not inappropriate.

Yes. In that sense, it's a perversion.

***

We are also told that Valmiki's grief at the sight of a crane being killed by a hunter, the grief which we associate with the birth of poetry, the elevation of a man transformed from violence into an ethical life, his gift of insight to all humanity, is really about the interruption of the crane's sexual act[4].

This is academia's equivalent of a pop culture genre convention. If you say it's about sex or violence, it's suddenly 'reality'. If you say it's about kindness and love, then it's ideology, Hindu fundamentalism, at that[5].

If you see the point of Valmiki's story as being about feeling pain at the suffering of another living being, you may not be academically fashionable, but at least you are still you. And if I may say so, you are still worthy of the pain it took your mother when she bore you. (That might sound like a Bollywood slogan, but it is not without reason that India's ethical sensibilities work in a melodramatic way).

We live in a world in which indifference to the suffering of others is an existential condition. It helps to think our gods and saints knew how to feel pain for others. We know too well in our own lives when others haven't done so for us, and maybe we haven't done so for them too.

***

One way of looking at what our epics and all our god-stories are doing, in simple, universal, modern, rational terms, is that they try to give us a sense of ethics through aesthetics. We believe, whether as myth, or history, or as something uniquely bigger than both, that poetry was born in the feeling of pain, not for one's self, but of another living being's.

Our stories may be reduced mostly to entertainment and commerce these days, but for us god is more than a superhero. We are at a time in our history when we are not yet sure of how to speak about our gods; we wish to believe in them now as heroes in history, and we wish to worship them now still as superheroes in legend. But even if we are fascinated by new ways of reimagining our past, even if we welcome newer and new age *gurus*, motivational speakers, evangelist-style *Gita* teachers, mythologists, spiritualists, experts (and textperts), we are steeped in the idea that *Rama* and *Krishna*, *Hanuman* and *Ganesha*, *Shiva* and *Vishnu*, *Lakshmi* and *Saraswathi*, all of them are our Gods.

We know them as Gods, and we feel them as Gods. We have not yet found the intellectual resources to speak of them that way though, in academia at least. Because academia, right now, is hell-bent, for lack of a subtler phrase, on proving that our god-stories are fiction. We argue, in turn, that they are history. Between these two positions, we forget the obvious. These are neither myth, in the sense of fantasy-tales for entertainment, nor are they histories, in the sense of what social groups do with each other. They are god-stories; a truly significant, enduring, and inspiring form of culture. God-stories are stories about God. We may not all agree that God is real, but we can recognize, in simple modern, rational, universal terms, that the social and cultural investment that has gone into these stories, into the meanings of these stories, is undeniably of value. For generations, poets, philosophers, patrons, audiences, parents, elders, women, children, sculptors, performers, singers, priests, farmers, workers, everybody, virtually has cultivated and embodied *an emotional and intellectual discipline* about the expression and experience of stories about God. We might speak about *Krishna* and *Rama* in many ways, but still, not in any old way. We might not accord the same cultural value or spiritual importance, or ceremonial reverence to every depiction of *Rama*, but we do place our sensibilities in honoring them. For example, some of us do not take books, any books, into the bathroom, still. Some of us might do so, but not books about God. We might not go to a temple only in traditional clothes, but we do still wash our feet when we enter. We respect certain codes with our bodies and lives because we know these practices are bigger than us. The stories we hear about the gods, the words through which we still remember them, these are like the temples and shrines of our culture too. There is only so much we can secularize them, and there is very little we can tolerate in their brazen and deliberate distortion too.

***

Academia though, is in some serious denial of what Hinduism means to Hindus, about what Hinduism means, in general. Confronted by the severity of the chasm between the decency of Hindu thought and its own vested distortions, it prefers to tiptoe around the question of meaning almost entirely. Instead of meanings, the Hinduphobic historian grasps some kind of an apparitional sense of texts, and illusions about the social and political conditions supposedly reflected in those texts. Doniger declares, for instance, that there is no proof of someone called Rama ever having lived or not lived in Ayodhya, but by interpreting the *Ramayana* in relation to its historical context, we can prove that is a work of fiction[6]. What *Rama* means in Hinduism is of course so vast that it seems almost a petty waste of time to respond to that. Typically, Hindus have believed that *Rama* was real, lived on this earth, and was an *avatar*, or God-incarnate. That belief was and is a part of our culture, a democratic, egalitarian part of our culture at that we can believe that a human being can be god. But we have not insisted that others subscribe to our belief either. Our faith did not need to coerce others into seeing things our way. But we have arrived at a point where the Hinduphobic compulsion to deny us our meanings has reached a point of absurd cruelty. If you are a secularist who disagrees, please try this exercise in empathy: if the collapse of the three domes of the Babri mosque could symbolize painfully India's tolerance, democracy and secularism crumbling (Dalrymple quoted in Doniger), if the symbolism of those domes was so sacred to secularism, to a 50 year old idea of India, imagine, *beyond the specificities of this one dispute,* in general, just how much more sacred the name of *Rama* is to the millennia-old soul of India.

The evisceration of our own meaning from our own culture is one of the most cruel, selfish, and hypocritical things that anyone can do. It is not that we are intolerant of other interpretations. We may not know there are 300 *Ramayanas*, but we do know that our one *Rama* can be spoken of, sung about, worshipped, or depicted in numerous ways ranging from the elegant to the near-kitschy. We have no problem with pluralism. In fact, given the absence of a social investment for nearly seventy years after independence in our educational curriculum to help connect our inner world of Hindu life with our modern ways of living and thinking, we are now ready to devour any kind of new knowledge about our past, even reams of names and trivia without an organizing principle or perspective. So what academics do, even reading the *Mahabharatha* and *Ramayana* as texts about the social conditions of the times would not be problematic for us. It is just that the particular ways in which Hinduphobia distorts these readings that have gone beyond a point of indifferent tolerance for us. We must learn to contest this intellectual challenge now. So if Doniger wishes to insist on ignoring the meanings of *Rama* and *Krishna* for us altogether to focus on the bards who supposedly told these stories, we must examine that too with an open mind. By the Mauryan age, we are told, India was a hodge-podge of many travellers, invaders, people, customs and tongues. No one disagrees with that, for we have no problem with accepting that our heritage consists of contributions of people of many castes and backgrounds. But the problem is with where this seemingly democratic rationalism is heading.

In essence, what Doniger claims, in addition to insisting that there was no *Rama* in reality and that the *Ramayana* is a work of fiction, is that the ideal of *Rama Rajya* was really a reflection of Ashoka's rule because the *Ramayana* was composed around that time. Whether the evidence to demonstrate another view is accepted in the near future in academia or not, one thing is clear. There is a strategic interest for Hinduphobes in denying Hindu agency. It is one thing to say there is no proof either way and let us just respect each one's beliefs within the scope of India's present laws. That would be civil. But it is quite another to now start to insist that the *Ramayana* was actually a fictional representation of the new progressive intellectual's favourite symbolic evasion from Hinduism — Ashoka. We see the civilizing mission theme speaking here yet again (it is a textbook move these days, also see Amartya Sen's *Argumentative Indian* for a discussion of how elegant non-Hindu Indian rulers were, namely Ashoka and Akbar).

But an even more brazen denial of Hindu agency, this time of women, takes place in Doniger's mythic opus. If the *Mahabharatha* had a fierce, independent heroine (as opposed to a passive one in the *Ramayana*'s Sita), Doniger writes, it was probably because the bards were impressed and inspired by the fierce and independent Greek women who came by to India at that time. Anything, even Aphrodite and Athena, can be dragged into this now, just to evade the reality that there might be some Hindu women who were fierce and independent too. This too is a common orientalist trope, an old racist colonial myth about the dynamics between white women and people of colour[7]. Rather than acknowledge that Indian women might have been independent and strong-willed themselves, a reality too many people know only too well, our experts tell us to salute the

---

We accord the status of an avatar to kings, cowherds, peasants and commoners. But what we do not do is project our flaws onto our gods.

independence of the foreign women who inspired Draupadi. The dusky Indian sexist male, after all, can only picture a strong woman when she comes from the civilizing West. This is but another part of the same race-addled imagination that produces, right now, on the most compelling TV series in America, the character of a blonde princess who enjoys being feted as a Mother Goddess by the dark-skinned slaves she has liberated. There is no denying patriarchy where it exists, whether in the West, or in India. But we cannot also deny the racial presumptiveness of the claim that Draupadi must have been inspired by Greek women.

***

There is much more that historians can question, even within the present paradigm that reduces all meaning to a reflection of social conditions, or at least a narrative claim about those social conditions. A great deal of the present 'alternative' historiography is based on presumptions and projections of present-day identities and subaltern claims into the past. At least some of these claims, as we can see with the Greek Draupadi charm, probably have more to do with unexamined colonizers' fantasies rather than fact.

Hinduphobic fantasies about history are one part of the problem. The more pernicious issue here is the somewhat hasty and bothered things Hinduphobic scholars say about our gods when they do get to them. In the absence of anything resembling empathy, or intellectual honesty (or an absence of hubris at least), it has become possible for scholars to make some incredible claims about the meanings of our gods against overwhelming evidence and reality. The issue here is not who the gods really are or were. The issue is very simply whether or not a scholar of religion has an obligation to examine his or

---

What we need now is a history of Hinduism, a history of Hindu civilization, and most of all, a history of life that is true to a Hindu view of it.

her claims with those of the scholars who live that religion deeply. From the very first chapters of her book, Doniger, adopts a hurried, dismissive attitude towards this point. Western Hinduism scholars are too afraid to offend the natives (or maybe she uses a politer word, granted), she says, but *not her!* That such a group called 'the Hindus' might even have anything in common seems to offend her worldview. Maybe *karma*, reincarnation, yeah, that stuff, maybe, but really, the Hindus have *very little in common* to merit such a term, she insists. This is the truth about the Hinduphobic position today. The very existence of Hinduism seems to rattle it so. At best, the integrity of Hinduism is acknowledged by a dozen words in a 800 page book, and that too, by throwaway words about vague metaphysical ideas at that, and not the one overwhelming reality Hinduphobia will not admit. This is the truth. Hinduism exists because its gods exist in the lives of its people; their names, legends, lore, local cadences, may vary richly, but the meaning of Krishna is probably the same to a Hindu mother in Kashmir as in Kanyakumari (and in Kamarupa as well as Kutch, as the new saying goes).

Our gods are peoples' gods.

Hinduphobia does not wish to see this.

With its fantastical speculations, with its bizarre claims about the 'violence' of the monsoon and our alleged permanent mental state of slavery to 'violent' gods, Hinduphobic scholarship fails to see the living, thriving meanings that people in India, rich and poor, of all sorts of castes, have for their gods. Doniger comes up at best with a half-truth when she writes that in our stories we see our gods as being just like us, seeking things like marriage, adultery and flattery[8]. In Hindu sensibility, the gods may indeed be like us, in the sense that we have a very egalitarian understanding of how the divine may also be human (or even animal). We accord the status of an *avatar* to kings, cowherds, peasants and commoners. But what we do not do is project our flaws onto our gods. The gods are like us, indeed, but only in the sense of *what we ideally want to be like,*

> Hinduism is a massively self-mastered attitude to the worship and veneration and indeed the adoration of the living divine.

aesthetically and ethically; not the other way around. We know God when we see God. Our gods may act like we do, but they do so out of their love for us. They do not crave adultery and marriage the way we do. They do not crave for glory on the battlefield. They do not crave for the pain of even their enemies. They do not crave, and that is what we are meant to learn.

The humility of devotion stands at odds with the arrogance of anthropocentrism. We can call *Krishna* a butter-thief, but we do so in the sense of an endearment, not a moral judgment.

Without that sensibility, we are not Hindus, and our gods are not our gods.

This is a simple truth that scholarship is yet to appreciate.

We are a democratic religion. Our pantheon never closes its doors. Today, even our temple, our community, our nation, if you will, does not close its door. Who has stopped anyone else from feeling Hindu, thinking Hindu, being Hindu, or borrowing Hinduism? Faced with a world of borders and definitions and me-first identities, we too now speak that language. But in our view of God, which is what religion is first and last, we are ever open. I do not become any less Hindu for offering my *pranam* to *Yeshu* or his mother, or *Allah* or *Yahweh* or *Guru* or *Buddha* or *Mahavira*.

It is our sense of devotion, our cultivated sensibility about what makes a god a god that makes us who we are.

***

What we need now is a history of Hinduism, a history of Hindu civilization, and most of all, a history of life that is true to a Hindu view of it. This is the work of generations of scholars, artists, writers, dreamers, visionaries, activists, and just children and new eyes and hearts to come.

What we have had so far is violence. What we have had so far is untruth.

By denying how we view our gods, our lives, our world as a whole, by focusing on fragments of texts shorn of their meanings, through distortion and delusion, Hinduphobia has created a fantasy of epic proportions. In today's academic historiography, oblivious to Hindu reality from under the fig-leaf defensive position of opposing fundamentalism, in this crazed denunciation of Hinduism disguised as an alternative, we see only violence. It seeps so deeply into the Hinduphobic mind that even the flippancy with which words, stories, ideas, interpretations are chosen and offered is not recognized and held in check. Our names, our gods, our words appear not on their own terms, but in translation, or rather, tangential mistranslation only calculated to insult.

A dog is not just a dog, but a 'Bitch'.

Shunahshepa the sage's son is 'dog-prick'.

The innocent blessing mothers and grandmothers offer to little granddaughters is related to a word that means 'having a long vagina'.

Can one say *'Subham'*, with all the kindness we feel in it any more?

Like the *Lingam*, another long story, translation without respect for truth is a form of terrorism[9].

Words are never only words.

Epistemic violence is violence.

> We are fed up of being told our gods are not our gods.

Doniger, by the way, describes the violence that followed India's partition as similar to the Vedic culture of revering violence[10]. In a rather contrasting style, we are told that the violence that came with medieval invasions and campaigns to destroy Hindu temples were done by 'nomads'. She also refers to the practice of breaking places of worship and building over them as no more than a kind of 'palimpsest.'

***

Whatever our flaws, and whatever acts of violence we Hindus may have done too in the past, our religion is still one of humanity's largest cultural investments in confronting the problem of violence.

The truth is we are as careful about force as we are about our gods. We are careful about everything. We are careful about how we portray our gods, about how we pray, about how we say the words we do, about how we hold the paraphernalia in our prayers and ceremonies, about which hand, which direction, everything. We may regulate these behaviours by telling ourselves tall tales of reward and punishment but at its core, Hinduism is a massively self-mastered attitude to the worship and veneration and indeed the adoration of the living divine.

The truth is that Indian civilization has not done to this world what the powerful colonial West did wherever it went for 500 years. Whatever its failings and flaws, for we are not above failure or moral failing, we have to ask if the critique we have for Hinduism today on issues like caste, women, and minorities, is appropriate, or even accurate, *in the form in which it is being done*. We need not shy away from self-criticism where it's right. But what we have been presented by Hinduphobia is no mere critique of Hindu dominance, such as it might be. It is a bizarre contradiction kept alive only by the power of postcolonial class, race, and epistemic privilege. It says: a) we don't exist, our religion is an invention and b) our religion is to blame for all social evil in India since time immemorial.

Which one is it then?

Only a completely false history of Hinduism can blame our religion for the problems in India today. It is the old trope of the Western civilizing mission, repeated again, and again, in various guises. It has lost its war, it has lost its colonies, it has lost its monopoly on our minds; yet, it does not recognize one simple fact. This world is not a kill-or-be-killed, winner take all, zero sum game. It does not realize yet that it can keep its gods, and we will keep ours. It does not realize that its problems with its gods and religions is not our problem with ours. But we will make that distinction clear. We can be teachers too, because we are unafraid to be learners.

We learn from the West after all its engineering, its efficiency, its linearity, its punctuality, its fast bowling; and we will continue to give it yoga, peace, the big picture, spin bowling (and now an inspirational baseball hero too it appears), and most of all a diet better suited for surviving global warming rather than the last ice age[11]. We have taught and learned from all the world for thousands of years. We know diversity. We respect truth and judge it by its merits rather than by secret political codes about the identity of who professes it. We do not simply pontificate it, and disguise our imperial rages with it.

The civilizing didacticism of Hinduphobia has to be seen clearly for what it is.

In the early colonial period, it was full of European missionary fear about false gods and demons; they are throwing people under the wheels of the chariot! They shout.

In the later colonial period, it was absorbed into the secular narrative of civilization and progress; the colonial subjects as primitive others, a concession of sorts made to Hindus that they were once Aryans.

In the post-independence period, during the years of the Cold War and Non-Alignment, that condescension took on a political tone; will India survive? Can the Hindus do business?

In the present era of globalization and neo-liberalism, the question now is restated as the rise of Hindu fundamentalism. It is the final gambit. By positioning the very non-fundamentalist, organic, liberal, pluralistic, *mainstream* of Hinduism as it is lived today, its temples, gods, prayers, and scriptures as fundamentalist, the discourse of the day has painted itself into a corner.

It either has to admit its defeat, or we have to live with the smear of being called fundamentalists forever.

***

We are fed up of Hinduism expertise that chastens everything we feel, think, say or do as something that it is not[12].

We are fed up of hearing *Ganesha* is a symbol of our fears of mutilation. We are fed up of hearing that our protest against the denigration of a beloved, wise, and child-like yet majestic sacred figure comes out of machismo and anger at his trunk being called a 'limp phallus'.

We are fed up of a world in which elephants were humiliated and killed[13] to please a pathetic human need for superiority, a world in which virtually every animal can be tortured and killed for superstition; either a known superstition like rhino horns for libido, or yet to be named as superstition superstitions like animals feel no pain or that we have no alternative to animal protein.

We are fed up of a world in which a philosophy concerned with truth, non-cruelty and love, and not with tribal wars and ritual slaughters, is systematically lied about.

> Hinduism does not believe God is the sole property of only a certain race of humans, or even the human race alone.

We are fed up of being told our gods are not our gods; that how our ancestors viewed God thousands of years ago was somehow very different from how we view it now; that in the past we were violent, stupid barbarians killing people to get rain and sun. We are tired of the denial of the truth that the Divine and its Adoration have been as deeply entwined in our lives as there has been life itself.

We may have called ourselves Hindus only for a few decades now. We may have had temples for only a few hundred years, or sacred verses preserved for only a few thousand years. But what we have at the heart of them all is something so old we can only say it is eternal. For Hinduism does not believe God is the sole property of only a certain race of humans, or even the human race alone. We do not presume to say we knew God before anyone else, because we believe God was being known, in all of life's forms, even before we humans stood up, walked around, and put a name for it. We felt it long before we knew there could be language, culture, philosophy, civilization around it.

Were we even human then? Were we but monkey-men? Were we life-forms of which even fossils have not been found? We do not know when it began, but we have felt this love, this existence, this truth, this beauty, this auspiciousness, for as long as there has been life. We have no words for all this. So we speak only of this history, this time since words began, or at least this time from which words remained still. *Vedopanishad, Bharatha, Bhagavatha, Ramayana*, whatever form in which we know these truths now, we can imagine them all over again as what they are; a journey in time, in God, to know God, in and through the vagaries and conditions of our times, our all too human, imperfect, unjust, cruel, uncontrollable, unethical, untrue times.

From Vedas to the Present, from Indus Saraswathi to the Present, whatever the markers of history we choose, whatever the names, maps and borders we imagine, a story of Hinduism has to be in the end more than a story of social groups real and imagined, and ruins and fossils and fossilized meanings.

A story of Hinduism has to be a story about god.

***

Part 2
SANATHANA
A Hindu View of God

Creativity is at the heart of Hindu life.

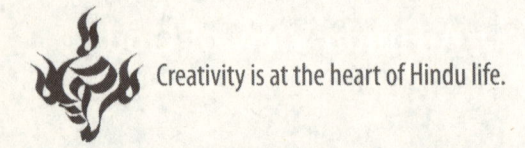

Chapter 1

CIVILIZATION: A PRELUDE

From Stone and Sword to Intelligence and Sensibility

We are living right now in a moment of vast civilizational hunger. It is not fundamentalism, nor fascism. It is an exceptional historical moment in which an entire generation of young, modern Hindus in India and the diaspora is growing up and asking only one pressing question: who are we, really?

Some of the responses to this question are emerging in our popular culture. India's biggest-selling novels in recent times are re-imaginings of myth and history. *The Immortals of Meluha* imagines the life of the Indus Valley era through the central character of Shiva, a fierce young man from the Himalayas widely believed by the more scientifically advanced people of Meluha to be the chosen Mahadev. *Meluha* imagines the sages of our stories as scientists, the gods and goddesses as humans, and the seemingly supernatural as reasonably explained through science. The great civilizations are splendourous, full of big beautiful buildings, and efficiently organized. Everyone is an engineer or doctor or manager (and of course, a warrior). Still, they are human, they are Indian, they are Hindu, because you cannot say they are not, and they are ethically engaged. They discuss things like good and bad. And they are intelligent, most of all. It is the biggest-selling book series in India.

Asura is a best-seller. It tells the story of *Ravana*, the villain of the *Ramayana*, sympathetically. *Ajaya*, an unusual take on the story of Duryodhana followed it steadily up the bestseller lists. On TV, serials about the *Mahabharatha*, and on the life and philosophy of *Shiva*, and the numerous tales of our gods come to life again, and again. The aesthetics get ever more creative (and unfortunately, digitally simulated, on the down side) but the sensibilities somehow keep returning to an ethical core. In a contemporary India angry about crimes against women for example, a TV production of the *Mahabharatha* cannot but present a special monologue by a furious Krishna condemning those who insult women.

It is the age when we want our gods as humans, and even our demons too.

It is also interesting that our new vision of who we are is emerging in the space of popular culture, and not necessarily from either academics or political ideologues. Creativity is at the heart of Hindu life. We do not have the resources yet to rewrite our history in a more accurate form. But our writers, film-makers, bloggers, and artists are expressing our yearning, and renewing a promise we did not quite fulfill with India's independence in 1947. We must therefore acknowledge one thing. The trappings of commercialism aside, innovation in Hindu culture is still coming from the people, so to speak. The conservatism and orthodoxy that liberals and progressives fear today is not the fault of ordinary Hindus, that much is for sure. Orthodoxy is at the heart of power, and these days we see it most in academia, and in the prestige media.

Aspiration, and hope, both belong to the people[1].

***

The new popular narratives of India's ancient civilization are neither history in the sense of real facts and events, nor are they mere bursts of cultural fascism as the Left might dismiss them as.

They mark the beginning of a new journey in the modern Hindu imagination. They are rooted in the present, in the experiences of a new generation responding in the form of creativity and entertainment to very real, global, national, postcolonial concerns. They are negotiations of today's world, of issues like power, corruption, the role of the individual and the family, the nature of duty, the ethics of means and ends, and the nature of good and bad.

They are about what our civilization might have been, and they are telling us even more about where our civilization is today, and where it is headed.

The truth of the present is simple enough. We want more. We want a vision that is rooted in the present, past, and future.

We want the missing links, between our modern school textbook history and our grandmothers' inner world of gods and talking animals.

We want a culture that is the best of what we know lies at the heart of our Hinduism.

We want our civilization back.

We want our gods back.

***

We live and think along a complicated timeline.

Cosmically or mythically, as they say, we have God and gods, always, everywhere, eternal.

But the problem, or the challenge, is that they are not just up in the sky. Our gods come among us, or we see some among us as gods. That is who we are, that is how our view of the divine is. We are

> We need to recognize now that even the terms on which we argue about history need to change.

pluralistic. We are egalitarian. We are democratic. We were this way before we even knew these words.

In school, we did not have to look for *Rama* or *Krishna* in a history timeline. We had a sentence or two about when the *Ramayana* and *Mahabharatha* were composed; who were the kings ruling India when they were, what wars they fought, and dates, of course, but not much more. We hardly addressed what these stories meant to the people, spiritually, ethically, and intellectually. Our curriculum avoided the most important questions.

In our mind, we therefore compromised. We could not accept that the *Ramayana* and *Mahabharatha* were only works of fiction or fantasy, in the modern sense. They could be art and Indian civilizational heritage, that was the best we got out of the Nehruvian consensus; but then they were also our own sort of scripture, we gave them that kind of reverence, and they were also accounts of our gods. We could not delete the belief that *Krishna* and *Rama* too lived on this land, somewhere, somehow; even if not every account of their deeds could be literally accurate or true. We developed therefore a cultural sophistication in the reconciliation of history and mythology, the divine and the secular, conservatism and liberalism, steadiness and change, one and many, on a scale even we lack the language to describe.

Today, under the stormy rumblings of a cultural and intellectual hunger that those who do not understand reduce to its one political face as Hindu nationalism, we plunge with heart, mind, rage, and still, love, into the worlds we have come from and we still live in. We begin our history anew.

***

Today, modern Hindus are seeking a better history for themselves, but the terms on which this history must be reimagined are not yet ours. For several years now, modern Hindus, especially young readers, have been trying to answer in their own way the denials and lies put forth by Hinduphobic historiography. That striving is not incorrect. After all, we have been told our past doesn't really exist in the way we think it does by the official historians, even though we can see it in India's landscape, its ancient temples, living and ruined. But confronted by the denial of our own voice, and indeed, sanity, by historians stuck in their own deep biases, we often turn our search into an inter-civilizational shouting match. We argue about our ancient glory, and how our ancestors had figured out science, engineering, medicine, surgery, technology, aviation, and administration a long time ago. Some of us do this consummately, and some of us do this somewhat naively, setting ourselves up for ridicule even though our intentions may be good.

We need to recognize now that even the terms on which we argue about history need to change. We need to go beyond those given by modernity, and by the commonsense parameters of pop historiography. When we look only at objects, gadgets, weapons and inventions as the markers of our past glory, we forget what else might have been too. We applaud for example, the granaries and observatories of ancient India, but forget that a whole worldview existed around them, intelligent, sure, but also intelligible to our ancestors in the terms that today are cast aside as superstitions and myths.

What we really need to do now therefore, is to understand how much more than gadgets and machines our rediscovery of the past has to be about. What we need to do is to step beyond the *template* of civilization that was given to us by colonial modernity, where, like in a video-game, we measure our greatness by how many war-elephants and cannons each army or empire might have had. What we need to recognize now is the invisible core of Hindu civilization, *its worldview* that is at once so vast and yet so careful in its attention to the mundane detail, and so protean and fluid as to seem ready to accommodate anything, but still able to return to its own moral core.

Civilization lurks in unknown places, in the smallest of things and gestures[2]. And underlying it is the largest of perceptions and philosophies. The real backbone of Hindu civilization is not something that can be seen in ruins or fossils, but in our commonsense, in our beliefs, in our culture, and how much it still upholds the changeless in a changing world. In our hearts, in every drop of whatever celestial chemistry that makes us who we are, we have one end to our stories; about the world, about life, and most of all, about God.

What we must understand most of all is our view of the divine. It is that which anchors everything else about us.

***

Given how old we are, and how diverse we are, it is only natural that no definition of Hinduism might ever prove adequate to its grandness. It is also understandable that we often define Hinduism by what it is not, rather than what it is; informally, we speak of a Hindu as someone who is not, say, a Muslim, or a Christian, or a Jew, or, sometimes, a Sikh, or Buddhist, or Jain. We also speak of Hindus who are atheists, and Hindus who may be thus entirely by choice and taste and not birth. Beyond this, there is little room for centrality and definition. We can accept histories of Hinduism that define us on the basis of our books (*Vedas, Gita* and so on), or on the basis of our spiritual leaders (Shankara, Madhva, Vallabha, Chaitanya and so on), or on the basis of our 'sects' (Shaiva, Vaishnava and so on). Somehow, none of these terms are adequate to our reality, because these definitions always put something other than our engagement with the divine first. These are modern conventions, and these are inevitably anthropocentric. These only

> With each generation, our gods and goddesses live anew, seen perhaps in the limited mirrors of the idioms and meanings each *desa* and *kala* gives us, but undiminished still in the hope and exultation they embody for us, that *sanathana* of love.

describe human beings and their deeds and legacies. But a Hindu view of Hinduism could perhaps look at something subtler, yet central to how we see the world.

If we truly respect the idea of *sanathana dharma*, the eternal way of nature, of reality, of the love or truth that 'holds it all together', so to speak, how can we also speak of how our spiritual culture has lived this idea through history? We have two models available now for our own Hindu historiography. The Hinduphobic one, which we have rejected in the first part of this book, is dubious. Our popular alternatives, the ones that are often dismissed as Hindu nationalist fantasies, in essence seek to prove we had an advanced past, brought down to decay by repeated foreign invasions. We should strive now towards a third alternative vision that does not see ourselves as either barbarians who should be ashamed or as victims who should be resentful. We could perhaps learn to recognize what it is about our philosophy that has helped us survive some difficult political and social conditions, which remain to this day, even if our stories expressed these insights as narratives about personal and familial dilemmas rather than grand geopolitical conflicts.

There is something in our philosophy that continues to survive, help us survive, and perhaps help the world survive too, relatively speaking, as we live through its most systemically destructive, forcefully stupid, and wasteful age in eons. It is not magic. It is not power in the sense of doctrine or dogma. It is only the fine art of existence embodied in Hindu sensibility. That is who we are, and how we have

> A better story, however, cannot be only about feeding our pride as we face globalization in all its forms, a mere "my civilization is older than yours" match.

been. We have been *sanathanis*, keepers of the eternal, not in some literal, cultish, mystery-novel sense, but only in the sense of knowing what is important, what is worth preserving, and what is better changed. We have not always been perfect at this. For whatever reason, whether it was inevitable or not, we do not know, but we did end up making ourselves conservative, clannish, and casteist at times. We might be making ourselves confident, assertive, and successful again now, with our support for strong economic growth and globalization, but without realizing fully perhaps the ethical, environmental, and social costs that might come with it. We might be accused therefore of being like chameleons, shifting our appearance to conform to whatever tide might be colonizing our habitat. But whatever life-form we are compared to, we are still the same. We do not see difference between the divine and this world, however, flawed and imperfect it may be.

What we must remember is this. We might want a better story of our past now, a more accurate history, because that is one need in our lives that all these years we were busy succeeding in science, engineering and medicine left unaddressed. A better story, however, cannot be only about feeding our pride as we face globalization in all its forms, a mere "my civilization is older than yours" match. It has to be about the present, and the future too. We are not a religion of dead gods, but living ones. With each generation, our gods and goddesses live anew, seen perhaps in the limited mirrors of the idioms and meanings each *desa* and *kala* gives us, but undiminished still in the hope and exultation they embody for us, that *sanathana* of love. Our turn to the past must be about that, about the duty we have to teach our children not just facts and figures, but the eyes to see beauty in this world, the heart to know gratitude and kindness, and most of all, the hands to build it all anew, ever more.

***

Hinduism is a massively self-mastered attitude to the worship and veneration and indeed the adoration of the living divine.

Chapter 2

TVAMEVA: YOU ALONE

Vedopanishad

A key question that Hindus and Hinduism scholars need to ask now is what the "origins" of Hinduism might look like if we were to go beyond the popular myths and ethnocentric biases that have coloured our imagination of pre-history and ancient world history. By projecting present-day territorial borders, identities and demographic definitions into the past in all sorts of contradictory and self-serving ways, Hinduphobic historiography has denied better ways of knowing ourselves. In this chapter, I shift the focus from geography and philology to sensibility; specifically, to the essentially Hindu way of seeing God as one and many. It is not a historic account of Hinduism as much as the recognition of Hinduism as a way of knowing that goes beyond the history of texts. And this way of knowing, in my view, has everything to do with knowing our place in nature, as its children, as children in relation to a mother, rather than from a position of domination over it.

***

Tvameva
Mata.
You Alone
Are Mother.

***

> Our Mother, for us, can also be just one generation away; our biological progenitor, or more broadly, this world itself, all that has created us.

In the beginning, for us, is a mother.

In the beginning, for us, is the love like that of a mother's to her child.

Hinduism's view of God is rooted not just in the texts and philosophies that come later in history, but in the love that all lives know.

Who or what it was that *first* had this love, we cannot say for sure. We might think of a particular divine being, an *Adi Shakthi*, or *Adi Lakshmi*, or *Aditi*, a Primal Maternal deity, but these descriptions are inadequate. When we worship, when we say *You Alone are Mother*, we are recognizing ourselves as a part of the living power of life itself, not presuming to stand above it and judge it as if it were but a machine, a chemical equation, and nothing more. We can be smart scientists when we put our day-hats on, and we can figure out those equations, that is not a problem. But it is when we look at ourselves in the mirror, or when we look at our children, and we notice, suddenly, that we are not just these bodies, these mouths, these pleasure-demanding organic devices. We think of all that has come before us. If we are lucky, if we have them still, we will think of our parents and grandparents and honour them, because in them we can see upriver to ancient eternities.

Our eternities are protoplasmic. Our origins are in life.

We cannot presume to know it, that one thing from which all has come, so we just call it Mother.

***

Our Mother, we adore in cultural creations of great exquisiteness. She is in the words of Shankara the Mother *Annapurneshwari*, life dancing up as steam from a bed of pure white rice. She is Mother *Shakti*, Mother *Saraswathi*, Mother *Lakshmi*. She is life and food and music, wisdom and friendship, justice and courage. We are not technical about it, but nonetheless we can always see our mother on her own, or also with our Father. We can call her just *Ammavaru*, Mother-Lady. When she is with *Shiva*, we call them *Adi Dampatulu*, Prime Parents. We can also call her *Santana Lakshmi*, or with *Vishnu*, as *LakshmiNarayana*, inseparably, auspiciously, kindly.

She is all the Goddesses we have turned to in surrender, men and women, for before our sacred feminine divine, we bother little about sex and gender. What we recognize is the enormity of life-power. We call it awesome names, and we call it gentle names too. We know. We know life.

Our Mother, for us, can also be just one generation away; our biological progenitor, or more broadly, this world itself, all that has created us; our food, our rivers, our trees, our books and schools, our society and culture.

Our origin-tales begin in a way without the need for leaps of faith or mythology. We keep our origins within our grasp in our lives. We touch our elders' feet, and we are right there, before them.

Our sense of origin is therefore neither the story of an invasion nor the fantasy of a fable. Our origin is neither a place nor a time. Our origin is life, and a sense of how we recognize our place in it.

***

The Hindu view of Hinduism cannot be appreciated in the dead terms of today's discourse. We don't reject science, and we can accept a physical view of our cosmic origins too, but what we know in our hearts and souls must also be spoken now. We must understand how Hinduism begins, in the best way that Hinduism allows us to do so. We must begin at the beginning.

> The popular Hindu view of Hinduism's past is not absurd, but just awkwardly stated.

In the beginning, modern Hindus are fond of saying, the *sanathana dharma* was everywhere; then, all the other faiths and religions emerged out of it.

We must think about this very carefully. On the one hand, it is a good sentiment, allowing us to uphold Hinduism's powerful philosophical capacity to recognize unity and respect diversity. A Hindu cannot really think that other religions are different in terms of the divinity that lies at the end of all worship and longing. For us, God is One but just known by many names. We believe God is One; and we know it is not quite the same thing as saying we believe in only One God. The tension between these two usages has existed between what we now call Hinduism and other religious cultures for a while now. But the question that modern Hindus now seek answers to is this: what was there before there was religion, in the sense we know it now, before what we call history? We reject the idea foisted upon us by Hinduphobic historians, but we have not yet expressed the logical possibilities of what might have been, instead. We have, for the most part, settled on one seemingly simple idea: we belong to the default setting for the world's spirit. We state it though, in the terms that modernity's limited discursive imagination has given us. We argue, often with embarrassing results, that the whole world was Hindu once upon a time. As evidence, we offer imaginative interpretations of language and geography; asserting, for instance, that California is actually Kapilaranya and was known to our ancients long, long ago. We are mocked, naturally.

Today's scepticism though only reveals a partial picture. When the sceptic's rejection of today's popular (non-Hinduphobic) Hindu history is itself examined, we could perhaps find better answers. We might find, for example, that the popular Hindu view of Hinduism's past is not absurd, but just awkwardly stated. Consider this. Hinduism has no founder, and no founding texts as such. We have an account of Hindu civilization only for about two or three millennia now, depending on whose historiography one subscribes to. The popular, emerging civilizational account of our past from lay scholars, writers, and others, pushes that date back a little further. But there is another possibility to think about.

What if the sensibilities that inform Hinduism go back even further than that?

What if the *sanathana dharma* really was the primeval and universal way of knowing the world?

***

Let us examine this possibility with a thought-experiment. It might seem very random at first, but let us play it out and see what happens.

Think of the last time you heard a cow call out. What did it sound like? Write it down, if you would like. (If you are an urban cubicle dweller and have never been near a cow, it doesn't matter, think of the word you use in your language for the sound a cow makes, or google it).

In English, of course, a cow supposedly says: 'Moo!'

In my mother-tongue, Telugu, a cow says: 'Ambaa!'

> We are speaking a language, and a language of the heart, that goes back to a time when human beings did not see themselves as different from the animal world.

Onomotopeic words are cultural constructs. A cow may not literally say 'moo' nor a dog say 'woof'. But consider one possibility here; even if for a moment it seems totally bizarre that a fairly sober book on historiography would be going down this pasture. Consider it, if only because your heart might agree with it.

How a calf calls its mother is actually not very different from how we humans call our mothers. In Telugu, it is 'Ambaa' and 'Amma'. The 'ma' sound, for 'mother' as we know, is common to many languages in the world, or at least the Indo-European languages. That fact, of course, is the sort of thing that those who believe in Aryan Invasions might like to state as proof of their belief. That is a different argument. But what we have to recognize is this.

We are speaking a language, and a language of the heart, that goes back to a time when human beings did not see themselves as different from the animal world in the way we have come to do so in recent history. The study of animal communication may be a recent science, and a laudable effort for the modern world to get out of the past 500 years of its anthropocentric myths that animals are not intelligent, or cannot feel pain. But what historians often forget is that humanity has been steeped in its bond with the non-human world so deeply and so long that we forget that this is where we must look to for answers about our own past.

It is also not coincidental perhaps that Hindus describe the cow as *Go-Mata*.

***

Today, our attitude towards the cow has become a symbol of some intense cultural politics. Hindus are told by Hinduphobic historians that we used to kill and eat them, until the Mughals decided to put an end to it. Hindus, in turn, end up making beef a central point of dispute in our relations with other communities, framing the issue not as one of ethics towards animals, but only as an attack on Hindu sentiments; in turn, other communities see this as an intrusion on their rights and have 'beef festivals' as a protest (we have obviously come a long way from fasting as a way of protesting injustice though). In any case, the important thing here is to respect not only the legitimate critique of casteism but to also somehow recognize the violent anthropocentrism that has come to mark our relationship to animals and nature more broadly today. Modern historians might include the analysis of nature in their sweeping stories, but rarely do they go beyond the assumption that the natural world is but a resource, a raw material, an object lying around for man's use and abuse. Hindu history, on the other hand, is better positioned to recognize where we have come from, where all of this human civilization as we like to call it, has truly come from.

We are already doing so, by asserting the place of the cow in our culture (though sometimes we miss the point of our ideals by using it a symbol to attack others). Faced by the contempt of sceptics, we defend our veneration for the cow by pointing out its economic value; how much more use a living cow is to us than a dead one. We point out how a whole way of life, sustainable, organic, grassroots, lives and thrives around it. Historians have also pointed out how much the opposite has also been true; much of the violence and conquest in world history for the last five hundred years, from the colonization of India and the Americas to the Native American displacement, has been connected to the rise of the beef industry[1]. Environmentalists are also warning us today about the massive costs to the planet of a cattle-slaughter based mass diet. These are all useful and important ideas.

But it may be the case that the most compelling reason a greater restriction on cow-killing was upheld in India than that of any other animal was perhaps not just its economic benefit, but simply because its suffering and death could not be accepted by the human heart even as much as those of other living creatures.

It may also be the case that the killing of animals was not as normal, widespread, or normative in parts of the world where

> In our lives it is easier to know *Tvameva Mata*, than just *Tvameva* at first.

climate and land permitted a less dangerous, less violent, and a less morally complicated way of sustenance.

It may also be the case that the abhorrence towards violence was more universal than our modern media myths about prehistoric cavemen hunters might have made it out to be.

In any case, to return to the main idea in this chapter: the idea of the cow as mother is perhaps not unrelated to the idea of *the divine* as mother.

***

The origins of Hinduism lie in a lot more than a mere ragtag bunch of poems composed by either bawdy horse-thieves or bloodthirsty hunters, as Hinduphobic fantasies about our ancestors imply. Hinduism is nothing less than humanity's striving to keep alive the cultural recognition that Life has been speaking to itself since the dawn of time. It still is. It is only modern human civilization with its fantasies about the dominance of man over nature (and women, children, and much else too) that has stopped listening.

But Hindu civilization will not let it happen any longer.

Sanathana dharma, for me, began whenever a living being held its young with love and affection on this great earth.

There was love, and kindness, on this earth, long before there was language, or even humanity. There were mothers on this earth, long before us. There was a vastness, an exuberance, an energy, if you will, that has not changed.

We began to give it names, somewhere long ago; in time, we looked back, and some of those names, we still revere as our Vedas, or, to be precise, our *Veda-Mata*.

***

Veda is *Mata*. It is our first teacher.

For us, the Vedas are not just how we feel 'about' God, but how we feel God.

The Vedas may name many gods and contain many more mystical insights, but inside all their richness though, even amidst all the gods they worship and adore, they are swirling around just one thing, the pillar of all their powerful mysticism; that is the idea of *You Alone. Tvameva*.

That one word, that elegant *Tvameva*, is the heart of everything. The Vedas may adorn that You in many splendid forms and names, enabling our surrender to the realities that make us who we are; the energies, the life-forces, the goddesses and gods, for lack of a better word than that. But in the end, in the beginning, in the endless beginning of the *sanathana dharma*, all of our striving is just that; to say, to feel, to know, and most of all, *be* in that utterance, You Alone.

It is easier said than done, for most of us. For children, for cows and their young, for elephants, for the living world in general perhaps, being in a state of surrender to the reality of things, being in nature, as one might say, comes easily. For us, as each one of us grows up, we must find it, either again, or for the first time, or perhaps at least come closer to it in this lifetime. So we begin, in our discussion in this book, in our journey through Hindu history, in our recollection of our own lives and biographies, with the obvious 'you', the most universal 'you', of Mother. In our lives it is easier to know *Tvameva Mata*, than just *Tvameva* at first, and it is only when we know that, when we know that love, can we strive for the love that then becomes unconditional, independent of the specificities of others and their actions.

Hinduism perhaps is always better lived first, and then understood; like any path of wisdom and spirit. Hinduism is often described as a way of life rather than a religion, perhaps, for that reason. We do not begin with a theory or doctrine that we then try to bend the world to conform to. We are, one might say, 'spiritual anarchists'[2]. We are ever evolving, ever free. Our constraints on occasion have been responses to history and circumstances rather than our own effort to impose our will onto others; in our philosophy, we have no Others, no reviled category for non-believers. We can be atheists, and Hindu. We can be monotheists and polytheists. But in all our freedom, we do, still, have a sense of a center of gravity; and that is the sense of You, Alone, around which we have created all our philosophy, culture, art, science, and indeed civilization too.

***

God is one. We say that. And yet we say that without insisting there is only one God.

We speak also of 330 million gods[3]. There are many wonderful interpretations of what that number means, what the gods mean. The one I like best says that there were 330 million people on earth when that phrase was coined. It just means each one is a part of God, each one is God. We do not separate. We speak of God, and of course, we speak of God in various forms and through various names. That sensibility, of God as one and many, is so deeply ingrained in the Hinduism that we know that we cannot avoid thinking of this as the core idea of our philosophy, even if the Hinduphobic historians argue that the Vedas were about random gods and violence. What we feel, when we hear the chants of the Vedas, after all, seem only to be supporting that idea; the *Purusha Suktam*, for example, seems to us to illustrate the idea that the One Divinity, God, exists in and through all the thousands of arms, legs, heads and bodies that walk around on this earth.

> The beauty that Hinduism teaches us to recognize is not outside the words Veda Mata has given to us.

Tvameva: You Alone

> From the beginning, there could not have been anything other than love.

But this seemingly obvious insight is denied to us in the present Hinduphobic academic approach. In scholarly books, the contents of the Vedas look almost unrecognizable to us in their obscurity, translation, and selective distortion. It makes us wonder, instead of trusting the validity of our own spiritual experience in the presence of our Vedas, if "that is what the Vedas *really* meant then". To some extent, we let this happen to us because of our craving for a modern, linear, chronological narrative. We look again and again to the past for some kind of authenticity on terms set by the present, not realizing that what we are witnessing is only an idea about the past, and never the past itself. We are pushed into imagining things that are not essential to the immediacy of the Vedic presence. Our usual imagery of the Vedic people is at least respectful, one of serene *rishis* meditating amidst gentle deer and bubbling waterfalls in the Himalayas. We are now on the brink of replacing that image which something else, something out of a barbaric fantasy. All of it does not really matter, as long as we recognize the terms on which these other stories operate. All of it does not matter, as long as we know what is and what was the heart of the *Vedopanishad*.

***

The term *Vedopanishad* is important. Our spiritual elders use it informally, and it helps us remember what is true, that the philosophy within the Vedas is no different from that explained in the *Upanishads*. But when we read the official history of Hinduism of the sort taught in schools today, we find a separation of Vedas and Upanishads across several centuries; this is done to sustain a political fantasy, that of the civilizing narrative. Bereft of the sound, sane, and deeply spiritual insight of the Upanishad that even

Hinduphobic historians can hardly deny, the Vedas are then easily distorted to appear as the seemingly unconnected primitive origin of Aryan Invasion Hinduism.

We need to break free therefore of the conventions of describing histories based on books, authors, invasions and superstitions. We must listen, as much to the chants of the Vedas, as indeed, our own hearts. The beauty that Hinduism teaches us to recognize is not outside the words *Veda Mata* has given to us. Language is not secondary to some external reality. Our chants are not orders being barked at nature to control it; such an attitude is a flawed modern, anthropocentric one. Our chants are what makes us who we are; and not just civilizationally or politically, but existentially. We need to listen to these words, to the meaning in these words. We may learn these meanings in English, or in other languages, but there is something in Sanskrit that speaks to us with an intimacy of the spirit that our modern tongues never fully translate.

Veda Mata is nature singing to itself in our voices.

The lexical evidence that survives, that on which all our histories are anchored, are no more than a couple of thousand years old, we are told. The words may have been only so old, but the lives that considered them could not have been so dull as to not have ever considered such ideas before. If we reject the modern myth of Hindu history as a primordial savageness civilized over centuries, then we see what really might have been a little more clearly. If we accept that the Vedas were not simply blood-chants, if we accept the spiritual insight, the love pouring out of their syllables, then we must also consider that the way of life that came before them had to have been vast, beautiful, so full of love for the divine that our modern mind can only guess at its richness.

From the beginning, there could not have been anything other than love. From the beginning, there could not have been anything else that one yearning.

Everything is Everything.

You alone.

Tvameva.

That is what the Vedas are saying to us, through us, in us, above us. They are saying, there is just one. You might think you are one thing, and then there are many other things in the world for you to react to. That is natural, and that is how we become as we grow up, more and more. But the truth is that separation is an illusion. Smallness is an illusion. Pettiness is an illusion.

Reality is possible, even with all its grandeur, its vastness. In the sound of our Mother Veda, in the laps of our own mothers, or in some corner of mother earth that has given us the blessing to call our own and our home, we can rise, in exultation. We can forget illusion. We can become something more than what our thoughts, and what our unsatisfactory circumstances tell us we are.

***

Vedopanishad.

God never changes.

We do.

The Upanishads, we learn about in our histories as commentaries on the Vedas.

Whether they really came only centuries later, or the seeds of their sensibilities were already present at an earlier period, is for historians to debate. But what is important here is this.

We can see a journey in them from experience to thought. Not unlike our own lives, from childhood to adulthood. In childhood, we don't just believe but we *feel,* Gods and God as real; there is no separation of belief and experience. In life, as we grow up, we outgrow its certainty, or at least re-formulate it, seeking reason, justification, history, science, for its presence in our lives. We enter the world of history and politics, micro and macro, to do this. We turn to our stories of the lives of our gods for our ethics, and even for our lack thereof. Then, somehow, through meditation, prayer, bhajan, yoga, seva, somehow; we seek the immediacy of experience again.

From experience to thought to action. And back again.

From Veda to Upanishad to Gita.

From childhood to adulthood, and the quest for innocent return ever after again.

***

The Upanishads call for no grand ceremonies, no philosophical disputations, no universities nor conferences.

A student is asked by his guru to mix some salt in water, and then to observe.

What then is this salt that is inside the water?

It is not visible, but it is there.

Like *Brahman*. Like the One thing that is Everything. Like the One thing that seems like many things.

What then is this?

Not just 'this,' but *that by which* 'this' is?

Not the eye, but *that by which* the eye sees.

Not the ear, but *that by which* the ear hears.

Not the word, but *that by which* the word exists

Not the prayer, but *that by which* prayer is.

Not you or me, but *that by which* you are you and I am me.

Not you or me, but *that by which* you can feel for me as if I am you and I can feel for you as if you are me.

Everything is Everything.

To think it is one thing.

To feel it is one thing.

To know it is above all to also be it.

Hinduism is sensibility, not doctrine.

It is what we feel, and not what the experts say it's about.

It is what we feel.

***

It is not surprising therefore that one of the oldest verses in Hindu life is addressed to the sun. Our modern minds may assert their narratives over our sensibilities, and reduce the past to some kind of primitive sun-worship phase in the march of progress. We learn the names of sun gods in various mythologies, and at best find it fascinating.

What our minds forget though, our lives still do not.

The whole of this earth still does not.

In the Vedas, God is Sun; self-effulgent, eternal (by normal human everyday conception that is), steadfast, upholder of all things, God's eye, Mother's warmth, Plant-Father, Food-Giver, Life power itself.

Every life form on earth recognizes the sun's rise each morning. Before the ages of arrogance and lethargy, before the confusion of sunless climes went into all minds on earth, surely, this must have been the one thing upon which to begin all prayer.

Tat Savitur Varenyam!

That Sun! That Life ... that Alive-ness! We Exult in Adoring You!

***

Once upon a time, long ago, the human experience, its culture, civilization, all of it, was simply rooted in a tiny mind facing a big reality; being *in* nature, so to speak, not presuming to be outside it, or above it. Now, in the modern, thought-filled world, it seems the other way around. Everything is layered over with our thought about it, our educated consciousness, our knowledge of it. Everything is mediated.

Today, we see the sun rise, but forget its stupendous awesomeness, its centrality, its eternity, its primordialness; in our mind, it is but one star among several million, and it will become a black hole soon.

What we *know* from our modern education fights with what we yearn to feel. Our religion does not deny our science, our modern world, but we have simply not yet made the language and idiom of modern perception fully our own. We used the language of science to speak about Hinduism so far, but we also need to do the opposite. We need to learn the language of Hinduism, which is not merely Sanskrit, or language in a conventional sense, but the fineness of a language, ultimately, of the heart.

Our understanding of the sacred is complicated by modernity too. We now believe more in process and procedure rather than the experience of it. We see *mantras* not as *nada-brahman*, sound as God, but only as passwords for god's ATM, for results, promotions, pleasures; and often, for escape from pain too. It is easy though to say that we must not use religion as a tool for our desires, that it is a selfish approach to God. But we cannot forget that all religion, all yearning for god, is born ultimately in a sense of powerlessness. We turn to God because we need someone to turn to. But what is essential, whether we see religion as philosophy or merely a habit of favour-seeking, is a sense of surrender, a sense of elevating experience over expectation.

Yet, we have come to prefer travelogues to the journey.

We seek knowledge where it doesn't exist.

We hold the light in our hands and wonder where the source is.

We are human. Where would we be without God?

Like evolution mimicking itself in embryonic development, like each life-form growing in its mother's womb from the shape of a fish to tadpole to mammal to human, each life in Hinduism is the history of Hinduism repeating itself. We feel, we think, we act, and then, we learn to feel all over again.

Veda, Upanishad, Purana, Gita.

***

The epics and the *Puranas*, for us, are not merely texts about the past but a perennial, living, cultural resource.

Chapter 3

COUSINS AND FRIENDS

Krishna and Rama

For many generations, Hinduism has unfolded in our lives not merely as an abstract argument about the oneness of God, but as a richly lived, felt, and celebrated culture of adoration for several divinities through whom we relate to God. We might have always felt that God is one, but it is in the recognition that God is also many, in the celebration of the many forms and names and the many deeds and lives of our gods, that we have also succeeded in living so well and for so long with so many different kinds of people and circumstances, and with nature too. We know God not only as Brahman, or Bhagawan, or Eswara, or Paramatma, but more popularly, as Krishna, Rama, and Ganesha, and with the kind of familiarity we associate with our own human loved ones; as parents, as children, as friends. The epics and the Puranas, for us, are not merely texts about the past but a perennial, living, cultural resource. Our stories about Krishna and Rama[1] and all our gods are not simply like lessons in a textbook for us (or unverifiable beliefs about the future or an afterlife), but an ethical template for us to find ourselves in, one generation after another. The present moment in Indian political culture has seen too many futile arguments about our stories though; so in this chapter, I offer not so much an argument about whether they really happened or what they really mean, but simply an impressionistic, devotional outline of how we feel about our gods, in close relation to the circumstances of our own lives and relationships.

***

Hinduism is rooted in one glorious instruction, which is to see all as One.

Tvameva.

It is an instruction ideally pursued in certain idyllic environmental conditions. In the forest perhaps, in the deer park perhaps, in the morning sun-bathed face of a Himalayan peak, perhaps; the sense of You, Alone is clear. There the salt and water dissolve, peacefully, like in the Upanishadic example. There, you are alone, a sage withdrawn from world and worldly mind. There you can be one, and become One.

But what of the rest of us?

What of all of us living not in forests, not in serene Himalayan lake hermitages, but in this world, this world of noise, anger, competition, desires, demands, and most of all, of people who will not be what we hope they will be?

We are put here in a social world, in a family, in a job, in a school, in a community. We are not just spirits in search of truth, but we are sons and daughters, mothers and fathers, brothers and sisters, cousins and friends, colleagues and co-workers, teachers and students, races and nations, even.

We are in this world.

We are here, as:

Sons and daughters.

Mothers and Fathers.

Brothers. Cousins. Friends.

Krishna and Yasodha.

Rama and Kausalya, Sumitra, and even Kaikeyi.

Parvathi and Ganesha.

Krishna and Arjuna.

Rama and Hanuman.

Between them, unfolds the universe.

Between them, unfolds all the love in the universe.

Ideally, we remember:

Tvameva

Mata Pita Bandhu Sakha

***

All life is in relation to its forms. All are children once, most become parents then, and like a swarm of bees descending on a flower-covered tree, millions of names, roles, forms, relationships, bonds, attachments, ties, loves and resentments come and go in this world. All life knows itself, somehow.

But we humans, we carry more than the moment with us. We carry history. We carry thought. We carry, to use a contemporary word, *baggage*.

Sometimes, in between two humans, a boy and a girl in love perhaps; or a mother and a baby in play, or an elder and a grandchild, what lies between them blooms full and true into the moment. It is love. It is truth. It is the sustenance of the cosmos. Baggage is forgotten.

But more often than not, in the daily grind of our lives, what lies between humans is not love. It is perhaps only habit, a social role, an itch or expectation, and sometimes, a prison.

Sons and daughters.

Mothers and Fathers.

Brothers. Cousins. Friends.

Between them, sometimes, also burns all the folly of hate in the universe.

Eviscerating Hate. Body-eating hate.

Hiranyakasipu hate. *Kamsa* hate. *Kaurava* hate.

Kingdom-scorching hate.

***

> Our perception of eternity is lived out not in cosmic terms, but simply in the everyday; in family, in generations, in time as we humans experience it.

In this jungle of our tangled lies and lives, in this wilderness of affections and attachments turned into recriminations and wounds, in this *samsara*, amidst shards of words and actions flying like pieces of broken glass, we do not see love anymore.

Still, it is from within this bitter brawl of family life that we Hindus yearn to find our Gods, our *Shiva-Parvathi*, First Family, *Vishnu-Lakshmi*, and our beloved Avatars, *Krishna, Rama*.

Our perception of eternity is lived out not in cosmic terms, but simply in the everyday; in family, in generations, in time as we humans experience it.

Mother, Father, Daughter, Son.

Brother. Cousin. Friend.

This is the way we know our gods, in the simple terms of the relationships through which we know our own selves.

We really have no sense of god outside the machine, so to speak, like a solo video-gamer sitting atop the universe with a long white beard (or a distinguished African American actor's voice) playing cruel pranks with our lives. That is not our metaphor. For us, god is not above and alone in that sense.

For us, god is always someone's someone.

Rama is not just Rama; but Hanuman's master, Sita's husband, Ayodhya's King, and most of all, that moment where it all started, Dasaratha's, and even Kaikeyi's son.

Krishna is not just Krishna; but Devaki and Yasodha's son, Radha's beloved, and Arjuna's cousin and guru.

Ganesha might have fought with his father, but he is still Shiva's son. And Parvathi's son, first.

Subramanya might have left in a huff when his parents scammed him on the race around the earth, but he is still their son too.

Their affections do not change.

They are our gods, are they not?

***

Every day, in virtually every Hindu temple on earth, from the most ancient shrines to modern ones, from Himalaya to Indian Ocean shore, and from North America to Australia, and even in tiny islands in between, in Mauritius, in Trinidad, in Bali, a Hindu temple invokes in its routines and ceremonies not some sweeping tale of cosmic creation but just daily life, just each day:

Wake-up time, God!

Bath-time.

Lunch-time.

Nap-time.

Bath-time.

Lullaby-time.

Good Night, God!

This is Hinduism as it is lived, none of that high theory, here. If we had to describe the core of our religion as it is lived, it is perhaps just these, the *suprabhatams* and *abhishekhams*, and the *naivedyams* and *prasadams*, most of all.

We do the same to our gods that we do to our own little ones, day after day, forever.

The expectation is of course, that we see them both as one, somehow.

That expectation is of course so high, only god can help us see him as god. As for the rest of us, parents, children, siblings,

> *God is not a mere theory for us, but experience.*

colleagues, employers, strangers in the street, characters on the internet, they are in theory, all part of that One.

But.

***

You, Alone is a near-impossible ideal for us to live up to given the reality of our human life; the human condition, we might want to call it. Given how imperfect we are, as sons, daughters, fathers, mothers, friends, rulers, citizens, we would have nothing to give us hope if our only chance at redemption or escape, or love, was not within the matrix of our relationships.

That perhaps is the most striking thing about our civilization. It makes sure that our gods are there for us in exactly the same terms we find ourselves in this world of *samsara* too; only better, only the best.

That is our sensibility. It is spiritual, it is practical, it is democratic and non-elitist, and not coincidentally, it is at the heart of a millennia-old explosion of art, literature, sculpture, music, dance and culture that is Hindu civilization's legacy to humanity's knowledge of the divine. There are few words we can find to capture all of the energy, all of the beauty, all of the truth and meaning that all of our culture has created around our sacred ethical aesthetic. *God is not a mere theory for us, but experience; and religiosity, for us, is not a mere apparatus to enforce some theory but instead a socially endowed practice of cultivated intelligence to sustain that experience.* We know only too well that our experience of god is only as good as our depictions of it; in poetry, in painting, in sculpture, dance, even comics and movies[2].

We could also call it 'mythology'. But we know what we mean.

We also know what we feel.

***

KRISHNA

For us, *Krishna* is not simply another character in a story, nor is he merely another hero who lived a long time ago and fought some wars. Our memories offer up many impressions of *Krishna*, from calendars, comic books, TV shows, cartoons, movies, a presence imagined in our hearts, a presence known intimately from our childhoods. In our debates, we don't always find the words though to express what he means; we speak, once again, on the terms set by modernity, to argue about history and archaeology, about Mathura and Dwaraka, but what we forget sometimes is the obvious. *Krishna* is neither mythological nor historical for us.

He is *Krishna*.

He is real. He is real when our hearts announce he is real, as great hearts, minds, voices, and artists have done so innumerable times.

Namma Udupi ... Sree Krishna!

He is real when we hear his name, in the voice of Jasraj or Yesudas, or MS or Bhimsen, or Balamurali or Chong Chiu Sen, or, in these new lands, in the voice of George Harrison or Krishna Das or Jai Uttal, too.

He is real when he hear of his deeds, again and again, in the words of Purandara Dasa or Chaitanya or Mira or Surdas.

Still he finds us, kind Krishna, little Krishna, he can't help himself.

He is real, most of all, when we see him in his sacred shrines.

A different adornment greets us each day in the holy temple at Udupi; sometimes *Krishna* is a baby, sometimes *Krishna* is a girl baby Lakshmi, sometimes *Krishna* is a tortoise, sometimes *Krishna* is a fish, and sometimes, *Krishna* is a mighty philosopher-charioteer.

Krishna. Our Krishna.

Stealer of hearts!

He will run home in your arms! He will enchant you, charm you, make you love him so much that attracted to that love he has put in you like a magnet, he will leap out of rock and pop into your arms and want to go home with you, maybe with a stop for cup-ice-cream along the way!

So they tell you at the temple; that is why he has to be kept locked up in the shrine, like mother *Yasodha* would. You'll see, when you go there.

Yet, like mother Yasodha knew, there is no holding him back. Still, he escapes.

Still he finds us, kind *Krishna*, little *Krishna*, he can't help himself.

He comes to each mother and father as their son or daughter.

***

And He stands, in life, disguised as rock.

He lives, in Udupi.

He lives, in Pandharpur.

He lives, in Tirumala.

He doles out food.

He doles out music.

He doles out wealth[3].

He is a giver. He is our god.

And if we ever forget that one most important thing, if we ever presume, with our human folly, to stain or diminish that sense of 'our', if we presume to deny His presence in all, if we exclude, discriminate, put our power trips and egos before him, *Krishna* will turn his back on those who do so. He *will* turn his back, literally, and smile upon his Kanakadasa instead.

***

RAMA

Did *Rama* really live? Was there really a God-King called *Rama*?

To say yes seems to get you branded as a Hindu fundamentalist.

To say no seems to be the only way to get you accepted as secular.

What does *Rama* mean now? What did *Rama* mean then? Is the question of what he meant then forever tied down to the politics of what he means and what he ought to mean now?

In our hearts, there is only one *Rama*.

Even if in our history there are *Three Hundred Ramayanas*.

And even if in our debates there are eight hundred philologers' pages of endless theses, erudite arguments, postmodern battles, political maneuvers, strategic essentialisms, subaltern recuperations, academic bush-burnings. This is the crux of all this agitation today, about India, about Hindus, about the world.

Our story. Their history. No one is more at its rupture than *Rama*.

History is inadequate; right-wing, left-wing.

The important thing is that history is still secondary, temporary. Today's history could be tomorrow's myth. What is eternal is prayer. What is eternal is devotion. We do not talk to *Rama* in the past tense. We do not talk to *Rama* as we would of any character in a book.

Yet, in today's cultural climate, two new stories rise up and run around each other like angry dogs in circles. One wants to insist

> Maybe that is why we yearn for *Rama Rajya*. It wasn't just about who *Rama* was. It was about *what He made us want to be*.

there was no such *Rama*, that he was just a character in a story, told and retold by all sorts of people sort of like modern day fan-fiction. One wants to insist, not unlike another kind of fan-fiction too, that he was real, but in the narrow sense of textbook history, trying to see in him not his infinite glory but mere fragments of facts and figures of dates, places, and conquests. We are loaded on facts now, but that is not the whole point; it is the *sensibility* that sustains them that we must cultivate once again, that sensibility which says, *You, Alone*, and adds, *You, Alone*, playing Your Dance of Games in forms we call mother, father, cousin, friend... even, enemy. How do we know You, then? *How do we live so we may know You?*

***

No ideal appears more often in our recollections of *Rama*'s life than that of sacrifice; he gives up the throne just so his father's word can be honored. He gives up his own beloved *Sita* to exile, after having been driven near-mad by her absence and after having fought a terrible war to bring her back. Today, we may find in some of his actions a powerful symbol to argue about, but the fact remains that it is as simplistic and anachronistic to say that Sita is a symbol of submissiveness as *Rama* is a symbol of patriarchy[4]. They might have been made that way, by lesser circumstances in history, on occasion, but to assume that we revere *Rama because* he mistreated his wife misses the point. *Rama* and *Sita* are both symbols, in the devotee's heart, for something more than what critics presume.

The sacrifice we revere in *Rama* perhaps is not so much of his own, or *Sita*'s, but of his own exalted status in his eternal afterlife as a God; somehow, while *Krishna*, *Shiva*, while all the Gods stand as Gods on their own and in their own form and image, for *Rama*, somehow, it is in the yearning of his devotees, in their greatness, that his own divinity seems entwined in.

Rama! Kodanda Rama!

King of our prayer-shrines, king of our hearts, king of whatever it is we consider the high point of our moral universe and hallmark of our civilization.

Rama, in Tyagayya's voice.

Rama, in Ramadasu's voice.

Rama, in Tulasidas's voice.

Rama, in the Mahatma's voice[5].

Rama, most of all, from the dawn of time to the unborn womb of future eternities, in the heart of that mystery, that compassionate infinity, that Mighty, that Monkey, that *Hanuman*[6].

Maybe that is why we yearn for *Rama Rajya*. It wasn't just about who *Rama* was. It was about *what He made us want to be.*

Yetha Raja, Thatha Praja. A *Rama*, a good king, can do that. He will make each one of us feel this land is ours, this world is ours, and we must be its guardians, its caretakers, its *sevaks*. He will do that. *Rama* is selfless. Selflessness invites love, energy, right action, justice. *Rama Rajya* is *swarajya. We rule ourselves, for the one we want to rule ourselves for*[7].

This is how we know *Rama*. History is incidental.

***

Rama's is the predicament of the good son, the good boy. Before the current fashion of deifying villains and anti-heroes in our movies began, perhaps we liked to think ourselves as following in the footsteps of the good son, the good boy, the good brother.

> All the gods and goddesses we know tell us love is possible. Still.

Rama was also the exasperating god, by contemporary standards. Why did he suffer so? Why on earth did he let *Sita* go? Why on earth did he let his stepmother get away with it? Why on earth did he exile *Sita*?

Krishna was smart. *Rama* was, in a sense, slow to react.

Yet, we know him, we know his suffering.

In the twentieth century, when most middle class Indians seemed to have been employed in the public sector, the deadly word we dreaded hearing similar to Rama's predicament was 'transfer'. In today's world, where professional mobility is seen as a good thing, that fear cannot be understood. Back then, 'transfer' meant punishment and exile.

And exiles have been inevitable it seems for our gods; from parents, from palaces, from kingdoms, from homelands and from beloveds.

Rama, Krishna, the two greatest, most beloved, most popular *avatars*; exiled cruelly; one on the eve of coronation, and one even at birth.

Even *Subramanya*, in a seemingly playful incident, cheated out of victory in a race by his brother and parents, flies off to go live on a distant mountain at the other end of the land from his parents.

At its core, at the heart of all of our stories of our gods and their deeds, what it is all saying is this, it is saying, *Look, God too can be un-loved; so if it happens to you, in your life, when your boyfriend or girlfriend does it to you, when your husband or wife does it to you, when your brothers and sisters do this to, when even your parents do this to you, when it happens to you, what do you do?*

When your own mother does it you, as *Kaikeyi* did to *Rama*; when your own uncle wants to kill you before you are even born, as *Kamsa* sought to do with *Krishna*; when your love seems no match for their power and their hate, what do you do?

Do you still find something in your life like love again?

If you can, what is it for? For truth? For *dharma*? Is it love for its own sake?

Rama and *Krishna* tell us that it is possible.

Hanuman tells us its possible.

Shiva tells us its possible.

All the gods and goddesses we know tell us love is possible. Still.

Love *is* possible again.

***

Mothers and Fathers.

Sons and Daughters.

Brothers. Cousins. Friends.

Krishna, the World.

The meaning of *The Mahabharatha*, maybe even the meaning of *everything*, in one concise interpretation:

It is not until one's relationship with one's self is right, that one's relationship with the other can be right.

Rama was also the exasperating god, by contemporary standards. Why did he suffer so? Why on earth did he let *Sita* go? Why on earth did he let his stepmother get away with it? Why on earth did he exile *Sita*?

It is not until one's relationship with the other is right, that one comes to one's own self, fulfilled[8].

The complexity of the stories in which we find our gods makes us think of complex ideas and ideals, *dharma*, for one. But in the end, it comes down to this. Our gods are not merely about our blind belief in magical or supernatural beings. Our gods are not merely symbols about either natural forces or political oppression. Our gods are *our investment* in the greatest meanings we can give to our existence and to our struggles as human beings. Our gods are how we know what it is to be human, for good and for bad, and how we can hope, still, for something better, how we can hope, for something like love.

***

Our gods are *our investment* in the greatest meanings we can give to our existence and to our struggles as human beings.

The popular legends of Vishnu as the *Dasavatar* are one way in which we still remember our relationship to the divine as nature.

Chapter 4

THE GREATEST LOVE

Dasavatar

"Cheema-lo, Brahma-lo ..." It is not only in the form of relatives and friends that Hinduism exhorts us to see the divine but also in the form of non-human life. From the tiny ant, to the vast cosmos, as Tyagaraja sang, we still find the same One thing. Without recognizing this key aspect of Hindu sensibility, its deep recognition of the sanctity of non-human life, we are left only with a shadow interpretation of Hinduism. Hinduphobic belief often denigrates the reverence we accord animals in Hindu thought as superstition and "animal worship," and at best, treats animals as metaphors for social groups. Modern Hindus must recognize that our "animal" gods are our most essential link to the living, natural world that modern anthropocentrism has cut our minds and hearts away from. The popular legends of Vishnu as the Dasavatar are one way in which we still remember our relationship to the divine as nature. In this chapter, I offer some ideas about how restoring our attention towards non-human divinities can help us better understand what Hinduism meant to our ancestors, but also help us critique and overcome the violent speciesism that underlies the environmental holocaust that has been unfolding across the world the past few centuries.

***

> We grow up thinking that the greatest thing in the world is to get what is being tantalizingly promised to us through our senses.

MATSYA

One day, when the world was about to end...

A fish saved the day.

"Why have You come in this lowly form?" The good sage asks Lord Vishnu.

Grace does not need to be preordained from atop hierarchies in Hinduism. We imagine our Gods coming down, from the sky, from the ocean of milk, or from the exalted mountain adorned by the crescent moon, but where they come, how they come, what they come into, does not matter.

In theory, in practice, all is His *avatar*. The salt in the water is also the salt in the body of all that lives. But sometimes, what is embodied is something more.

Whether there was really a talking fish that grew to epic proportions in just a few days is not the question. Whether there was really a turtle that lifted a mountain is not the question. Whether there was really a Rama or a Krishna or a Hanuman is not the question. Whether there were some local heroes who got elevated by the circulation of bardic tales into a mythology of divinities is also not the question, it is in fact, a distraction.

The question is simply this: would you call a fish a god if, somehow, in the improbable but not impossible array of causes and things, somehow, it helped you?

Or would you only see the lowly fish?

***

It is the greatest love.

It can swell a tiny fish to the size of a continent-hauling whale.

It can make a God swallow all the world's poison in one gulp to keep life safe for us.

It can call a God out of a pillar, in a flash of fire and clap of thunder, a god who is half-lion, half-human, fully smarter than any conundrum or condition raised against him.

It can also wage war, and it can suffer, for love.

It is God. It is devotee.

It is inevitable, though its seeming impossibility is about all we think about.

As *Yudhisthira* tells the *Yaksha* of the Lake, what is inevitable is not death, as we often think, but happiness[1].

We live of course, in the age of the greatest industrial scale output of happiness ever made, or at least so we are told. From the time we are born, advertising, consumer culture, consumerism-based parenting, everything tells us this world is here to buy happiness from. We grow up thinking that the greatest thing in the world is to get what is being tantalizingly promised to us through our senses; to get whatever we think will give us ever greater physical gratification and pleasure. The shop is therefore the metaphor of choice for all we desire today. And for those of us fortunate enough to afford entry, we have no end to what form we can buy happiness in; toys, clothes, candy, ornaments, cars, gadgets, pictures, drugs, status, power, prestige, whatever it is. We live our lives working, wishing, scheming, if necessary, for this.

> We will need eyes to unveil a greater illusion than what our ancestors might have needed to look beyond.

How do we learn to look at truth again?

But we wonder sometimes if we really are happy. We wonder if we are doing what we are really here for. We wonder if our love is real.

We wonder still if the greatest love is possible, in today's world.

We don't have answers for that. We might find some answers at best only for what is wrong with today's world using the limited language our discourse gives us today. We recognize at best problems like corruption in the government, and stress in our work and lives. But we seek, still, the language with which we can name what we want to find more than anything else in this world. For something like the greatest love to be understood, we will need eyes to see what ails this present world far beyond corruption and stress. We will need eyes to unveil a greater illusion than what our ancestors might have needed to look beyond.

***

Is the greatest love only a myth of the past? Or was there such a thing for real?

Was it love that brought the Great Lord *Mahavishnu* Himself down to earth?

Or, even within the terms of reason, one might ask: was it love that elevated ordinary men and women into saints?

What was that love? Was it selflessness? Was it its unconditional existence, free of expectation?

Is there a name for it? Or a technique for it?

How do we get it? Now? Is there a shop... perhaps?

We might ask the question now, for this is a book, after all, about God.

Is God real?

Or is it all just how we look at it?

If so, how do we learn to look at truth again? In practical terms, what is it that we need to recognize in order to better understand the question of God, or at least, the possibility of love in this world? Are the secrets hidden in our ancient languages and in the ruins and relics from our past? Or is it all right here, in plain sight, in our lives, in our customs and values, mixed up, but still holding the promise of showing us a way forward?

Is the greatest love right here, right here now, all around us, in the world that is living all around us, in every ant, fly, bird, and beast we see, and is it only our limitations as human and socialized beings that deter us from grasping it?

Perhaps it is.

***

The world we live in today, the modern industrial, or post-industrial world, is based on a very specific culture's assertion of the dominance of the human species over all else. It has brought us great benefits and pleasures, no doubt. But each day in the life of planet *homo* not so *sapiens* today carries the *karma*, so to speak, of the massive destruction of millions of living beings around the planet. Recognizing this should not make us defensive. The answer is not to say either drop out and be a hermit, or continue to ignore this. The answer is to merely learn to see it for what it is. What we have to acknowledge first, is just one simple thing.

> Are the secrets hidden in our ancient languages and in the ruins and relics from our past? Or is it all right here, in plain sight, in our lives, in our customs and values?

How the modern anthropocentric mind sees nature is not the only way of seeing it. There is a greater insight in nature's theater, in the theater of life, so to speak, that our modern discourses about nature, life and animals, can only teach us so much about.

It is nature, ultimately, that we will have to turn to once again, *to know what it is to love, and be loved.*

It is only in nature, that perhaps we will know what it is be not just Hindu, or human, but in the *sanathana dharma* itself.

***

The *Dasavatar* is one way of offering a sense of narrative on the fundamental core of our philosophy: that all life is divine, God is in everyone and everything that lives.

Evolution is science's way of telling that story, in the language and in the power trips of science. Unlike in places where both science and religion face off as power trips, in India there has been no conflict between the two.

A Hindu still sees a monkey and says *Hanuman*!

A Hindu still sees an elephant and says *Ganesha*!

A Hindu still sees an eagle and thinks of *Garuda*. A Hindu still sees a snake and thinks of *Subramanya* and *Shiva*. A Hindu sees God, still, in the vast world that the modern way of life has learned to ignore, suppress, and devour.

A Hindu still sees God.

A Hinduphobe only sees a primitive animal worshipper in the Hindu.

Actually, it's something much worse than even Hinduphobia that denies life its own integrity. It may not be the Greatest Hate, but it is certainly the Greatest Delusion that plagues the human world in our time.

How many more PETA celebrities must try before we recognize too many have died?

Yes, and how many slurs will we face before they know, *this is what we have said all along?*

***

Despite what the media and pop culture tell us, in reality, it is not always natural for human beings to feel remorseless about killing[2]. Steeped in the greatest love, as we believe all life is, we would not have been able to live by taking life; especially life that cries just like us in pain if you slaughter it. The separation of life into human and animal[3], and the assumption of an attitude of unrelenting supremacism is nearly impossible for a human being without the invention of a vast mythology of anti-love, a vast and deliberate ideology of denying to non-human life what we know in our hearts and through our senses to be quite true.

The 'silencing' of animals was perhaps the only way to overcome the remorse that nature's intelligence makes us feel. Some of the great myths of religion too have been interpreted as metaphors for the horror of killing animals for food[4], to the shame of hunger which forces man to dominate over life itself. *That* is an end to innocence.

For the great slaughter to begin, there had to be a great silencing first.

To find extra strength for that silencing, for the human heart is no different in the West or the rest, propaganda had to be invented to further mystify the ugly noise in the anthropocentric mind.

First, it was the pseudo-religious propaganda about the inferiority of animals.

Second, it was the pseudo-scientific propaganda about the non-sentientness of animals.

I think, therefore you are a machine and feel no pain. Thus cogitated Descartes[5].

They beat dogs to death and laughed. "Their cries are not of pain", they said, "Just the sound of a machine, like a door squeaking".

It is that kind of cold cool cruelty that pervades the world today in the name of science, progress, and modernization.

And of course, *things we pretend don't matter about animals, we soon stop caring about ourselves too*[6].

***

It is probably more than coincidence that in the *Dasavatar* Lord Vishnu appears in some of the key forms that evolution tells us we came from: fish, turtle, mammal, humanoid, human[7].

But inadequate, intemperate, uninformed, modern day critics repeat after each other: it's either evolution or creationism.

Bruised with its science wars and its culture wars, the young civilization of global modernity scrapes together consciences and histories and starts to glance out hesitantly from its navel outward to its peripheries. After three centuries of enshrined Eurocentrism, after the myth of the Hellenic-Christian miracle, it hears some voices from its borders.

Better for it, it now acknowledges; we were your poor cousins, O Mesopotamia! We got our numbers from you O Arabia! And thank you for the gunpowder, ancient China.

Bruised with the greatest salvo of its culture war, one that has not even really ended, despite a million pieces of plastic dinosaurs littering the childhood landscape of America, it holds on somehow to Evolution.

Suitably, it also begins to admit that evolution was somehow figured out before Darwin by an Arab scientist[8]. Like the zero, like science, the West, or at least its liberal fringe, now eases its conscience about past appropriation by admitting to the existence of civilization on its powerful borders. It can cede some credit to its Arab brothers who gave it math and astronomy and civilization, and even evolution. But not much further though. It cannot say the "H" word. It cannot even say the "I" word, for that matter, still listing us as "*East* Indians" on its government forms.

Meanwhile, in India, in modern, 21st century culture-war India, a progressive art house announces that it will host a talk by scientists on the Scopes Trial so that people can come and get over their creationist superstitions about Vishnu and Brahma.

In the words of an American saying, we might want to say, Go Fish.

***

Evolution understood life better than what the culture that spawned it had done before. It answered the question of who we are better than anything its philosophers had offered. Faced with unrelenting prejudice and superstition, still, it survived, a triumph of reason over superstition.

Yet, it remains trapped in the language of its making, in the imagination of a greater ethnocentrism that denies it the poetry life sings in.

In the popular narratives of our time, evolution appears impersonal, a calculus of survival odds, struggle, imagined invariably in tales of bloodied violence. We must remember one thing about its origins. It showed up in the history of human thought just when someone needed an excuse to justify the slaughter, not only of animals, but also of the colonized world. It fit nicely. Survival of the fittest. Predator and Prey. Stronger nations and weaker nations.

> We recognize *vatsalya* everywhere, and in our art, we depict it as much in the animal world as the human one. Our *Hanuman* is still the son of *Anjana*. Our *Ganesha* is still the son of *Gauri*.

Evolving racial species, and an evolved race; or "developing" nations and "developed" ones.

At one level, evolution is narrated in today's pop culture as little more than an evolution of killing power; T-Rex Teeth, Stone Age Spears, Gatling Guns, Atom Bombs.

That's one way of looking at things.

***

In America, evolution and creationism are both subsumed within its own peculiar cult of survivalism. Beyond the great California spiritual promise (and that is only said half-jokingly; to say it fully seriously would be naïve, and to say it fully as a joke would be cynical if not suicidal), most of American pop culture still cannot imagine a past outside of hunting and killing. Its nostalgia is for something called a paleo-diet. Its hit reality shows are about duck hunters. It addresses health problems accruing from eating too many hamburgers by declaring war on carbs and throwing out the bread instead of what is between. It is survival of the fittest in Red, White and even some Blue.

Evolution has been widely understood in the modern world, like much of life, on the terms of a machine model. Without a sense of wonder, a sense of the greatest love that exists all around us, it becomes a justification for the violence and injustice of the status quo. We call it Social Darwinism when it gets exceptionally nasty in the realm of human affairs.

We have no name for it yet when it comes to excusing the nastiness that exists today in the domination of animals by human affairs.

***

Evolution did not disturb Hinduism greatly, in fact not at all. Modern Hindus naturally are proud of noting that the *Dasavatar* proves that the ancient sages of India were scientifically advanced and predicted the discovery of evolution before Darwin ever did.

> You will not forget that somewhere, somehow, your grandmother taught you, even if your science teacher didn't, that your pleasure cannot be truly pleasurable if it is rooted in the pain of another living being.

At the moment, our present knowledge encourages us to be sceptical about that.

But what we learn tomorrow may outclass our scepticism too. It seems to happen that way with Hindu history, for this is a project that is just beginning.

The important thing though about Hinduism and evolution is not who invented what, but simply the fineness of perception in our thought that can illuminate it better. We recognize *vatsalya* everywhere, and in our art, we depict it as much in the animal world as the human one. Our *Hanuman* is still the son of *Anjana*. Our *Ganesha* is still the son of *Gauri*.

We know it all, still. Even in our movies, especially the older ones, when we saw birds, flowers, trees substituting for human emotions and actions; we laughed, thinking it was Indian prudery, avoiding showing a kiss by cutting to nature. True. But that wasn't the only thing. Our popular culture was reminding us about our place in nature, still, even if in all sorts of funny, convoluted, melodramatic, and commercialized ways.

We were critics of the froth, but we forgot we were also swimmers in depths.

***

Hinduism still invokes a sense of the greatest love. Our tales may be jumbled up, complex, contradictory, changing, even chaotic, a postmodernist's delight; but they are not devoid of feeling, a feeling rooted in clarity of purpose. The end of all our stories, the avatars and the miracles, the wars and the little charming ditties, all of them, somehow is to bring us back to that wonder, that surrender, that recognition of *Tvameva*, and not just with the human world alone.

Even if the modern Hindu doesn't always act that way in a zoo, or in a street with stray dogs, or in a modern food ecosystem with non-cruel choices, the fact is that the worldview of which we partake today doesn't forget what is what.

The failure of morality is another issue, and we will confront it.

But the sensibility in which life exists in Hinduism cannot be smirked away.

***

We do not believe that humans have a monopoly on God.

One might say we believe animals, indeed all creatures, have souls; and typically, our actions in life lead our souls into higher bodies until one lifetime at last, we escape.

But 'souls' are not the only way of looking at things now, in the modern world.

In less metaphysical terms, perhaps, what we are doing is recognizing everything is connected in nature.

Could you, for example, kill a cow if its playfulness with its calf reminded you of your mother's with you when you were young?

We could once again argue that it's a kind of anthropomorphism, that we project our human feelings and ideas onto animals, like a Disney movie. But it may well be that this is how the Indian mind has experienced, and given meaning to life. You are always small before Life. You are always small before the vast galaxy of voices, small and big, that surround you; human, animal, bird, insect, even microbe. You give it all names, temples, mythologies, stories. You do not presume to put yourself above it, beyond a point. You may allow for human need to swell to the point of even greed, but you will not forget that somewhere, somehow, your grandmother taught you, even if your science teacher didn't, that your pleasure cannot be truly pleasurable if it is rooted in the pain of another living being.

One of the biggest transformations in modern life is the near complete removal of our ability to recognize the living among us. We have a discourse of rights that helps, to some extent. But what we have nearly lost in the modern world is the capacity for compassion as a human, indeed biological, imperative.

Our education, our mediated life, all of it clouds us over and distracts us from the one overwhelming reality even critics and poets and revolutionaries seldom manage to be heard against. The world today, this massive edifice of civilization, its buildings, roads, ships, factories, malls, gadgets, everything has been built not just on the stolen labour of workers and women and subalterns and peasants, as academics and activists warn us, but more literally so on the blood of countless billions of living beings.

The muscle that it takes to run all this has come cheaply for us, but at great cost to others that live.

We humans did not have to kill to eat anymore, unlike the eagle or the tiger or the hyena.

Yet, we still do.

And we humans kill each other too, massively. Simply. For lack of imagination, want of alternative, absence of freedom, greed, money, pride, and many times, simply, for pleasure too.

How can we ever learn not do so?

Only the greatest love will teach us.

Only seeing the greatest love again, right here, in this world and in this life, can teach us.

***

We are speaking a language, and a language of the heart, that goes back to a time when human beings did not see themselves as different from the animal world.

Chapter 5

TEACHER

The Gita

At several important moments in Indian life, the Bhagavad Gita has been the central text that we have turned to for answers to the question of what we must do. In this chapter, I submit that the Gita might be approached by us not only as a guidebook for personal success and spiritual growth but really as a social wake-up call against untruth, injustice, and a world going wrong as a whole. To put it in the context of our narrative in this book so far, if Hinduism recognizes that God is present in the love that exists in all beings, human and non-human, then the Gita is our way of asking the divine as Guru how we might live that recognition best in our own time and place in history. And what Guru gives us ultimately is not just mystical or magical vision, but the gift of truth, reason, and understanding that will help us recognize the vast complex of causes and effects that produce this moment, this world as a whole in this moment. The Gita's profound image of the vishwa-roopa-darshana, for me, is a way to see the relatedness of everything as a whole, in whatever form our hearts and minds, our personal idiosyncracies and idioms of meaning, our own intellectual and cultural dispositions, will allow us to witness.

***

So what is it that *Krishna* taught *Arjuna*?

So what is it that we have taught ourselves, again and yet again, one generation after another, one challenging phase in history after another?

And we were doing this for quite some time by the way; we were living Hinduism quite steadily even if we didn't call it that for far longer than the Hinduphobic historians assert.

Our vision, our visionaries, were steady, vast, and each of their lives, each of the lineages of thought, discipline, practice, and service they established has lived on for hundreds of years now, influencing the course of millions of lives, directly and indirectly.

We live now in the land and the legacy of the three great teachers.

Shankara, Ramanuja, Madhva[1].

We live in the gift of the more recent message, for our times, about what we must do to live, and live in life, even in the face of monstrous ignorance.

Sri Ramakrishna, Vivekananda, Ramana Maharshi, Yogananda, Aurobindo and in my view, the *Mahatma* too.

And then, a mystery, among many secrets and mysteries of grace, love, and sacredness that appear rapidly all across this still-holy land; the *gurus*, the *avatars*, the beings whose presence is as universal, varied, local, democratic, and yet vibrant as Hinduism itself.

Sai[2].

Many, many great ones!

Endaro Mahanabhaavulu!

And from them to you, to me.

To all of us.

Krishna lives in our hearts and in our lives in ways that cannot be explained away.

Krishna never did get off that chariot. If he did, he said, the terrible and destructive weapons unleashed on his dear ones by their arrogant enemies would slip out from under his toe and destroy everything.

Long ago, there might have been one *Krishna*, one *Arjuna*, one event. Since then, it has all been in our heart, so steadily and vividly in our heart, that we cannot only think of *Krishna* as just a man who lived and went long ago. He is an *avatar*, a divinity. Our minds can explain this in whatever way our modern sensibilities permit us to. But the fact is *Krishna* lives in our hearts and in our lives in ways that cannot be explained away[3].

We are here, now, hesitant, confused, the rest of each of our lives spread out in front of us. Choices, possibilities, questions, doubts; what to eat, what to tweet, what to wear, what to care about, what to study, where to work, who to love, who to marry, where to live, who to believe...

If you are young, a young *Arjuna*, then *Krishna* is perhaps speaking to you as a parent, or an elder you trust.

If you are old, an old weary *Arjuna* fighting battles again and again, then *Krishna* is speaking to perhaps as a *bala Krishna*, a young one, your child or grandchild, in innocence and freshly baked from God, showing you the way.

If you live, *Krishna* is speaking to you as your conscience, your inner voice. He is the Eternal Witness. He wants you to take the reins of your own lives, your own thoughts, words, actions, in hand. He wants you to start doing and to take pleasure in doing that which He is here to do always, again and again, *sambhavami yuge yuge*.

He acts, through us. We are all His *Arjunas*. But only when we are in *dharma*, in truth, kindness, unselfishness, love. That condition must be respected. Otherwise, we might be blaming *Krishna* for our own faults and failings[4].

***

Is the greatest love possible in this life, our mundane, mean, meaningless life? What is it? What is it that *Krishna* revealed to *Arjuna* on the battlefield? Is it different from what the Buddha saw under the Bodhi Tree? Was the difference only one of cultural perceptions of authorship — in Hindu sensibility we saw it as a gift from God, and in Buddhist and more modern sensibilities just the accomplishment of human striving, the end of a compassionate human being's struggle to really see?

What is it that we are meant to see? Unity? Selflessness? Emptiness? Love?

"Wow, look at the world!" as a three-year old boy used to say, even when he had just started to speak.

Are we meant to see Wonder?

No words are adequate to the great goal of all teaching, the end of all our striving[5]. We think *Moksha*, the Great Escape, must be grand, final. So we think, perhaps, of the meaning of all this life and effort as but a way to find some preordained escape velocity from cycles of *karma*. We think, perhaps, it is what we can hope to find when the clerk who stands by the side of the demigod of death clears his throat and reads us the account sheet of our life's actions.

But is this end of all our striving, this great escape, really about the end?

Or is the greatest love really only about all we have known in the end that is really in every moment?

Every moment a battle field, a hesitant you, a hesitant me, urged on by some mental template *Krishna*, cousins, friends, elders, gurus,

---

But perhaps you have seen your rock in your *sanathana dharma*, and somehow seen it live well and adapt to the requisites of *desa* and *kala*.

pop culture heroes, gods, DNA, destiny, stars, *Guru-Balam* in the right position?

Every moment a decision: to act, not to act.

If you have set your life in order, if you have been reasonably committed to *purushartha*, done your studies, guarded your health, secured employment and home and means to live, found friendship in marriage, and perhaps even made the blessed journey of parenthood, been blessed to journey that is, from having once been someone else's, as a child, to becoming independent, and then sacrificing your own supposed illusion of freedom to the serene surrender of belonging to someone else now, to your children, most of all, then perhaps your *dharma* is on autopilot now. Things might and things will rock your ride, still, just when your teens have ended and adulthood is here; parents, age, health, most of all.

But perhaps you have seen your rock in your *sanathana dharma*, and somehow seen it live well and adapt to the requisites of *desa* and *kala*. Maybe you are an American Hindu. Maybe you are a new age Hindu, or a *yogi,* a Hindu by thought rather than name. Maybe you are this, or you are that.

But who is this *Krishna*, this God, once whom you adored as child, your child and every child, but is now also the God the charioteer the manifesto-maker for war; is it is his breath that still wafts down the protoplasms of our ancestry to give us now these thoughts?

Flute calls are what we hear in life, when *Krishna* is in Vrindavan, in our lap.

Conch shells are what we hear in life, when we have to face it. Because even *Krishna* had to leave his childhood behind.

And we do too, every day, in so many ways, in ever new ways. Troubles do not end.

And neither do lessons.

***

The Bhagavad Gita, the Song of God. The teachers teach us its perennial wisdom again and again, in ways that make sense most to our *desa* and *kala*, to our place and time in history.

Five heroes versus one hundred enemies.

Five senses.

One hundred enemies to usurp those senses.

In today's mass media inflated cultural environment, one hundred is a modest figure. It is more like thirteen hundred channels of filth and a trillion websites of the same to choose from.

Five senses.

One *Krishna*[6].

One supersoul in which all we individuals feel the illusion of separation, go through life and its story thinking I, we, mine; thinking, *my* soul, when all there is just One, daring you to live up to it in and through and past your mind.

One *Krishna*.

***

In its simplest interpretation, the *Bhagavad Gita* may be seen as a call to war. Within the story of exiled and cheated cousins, and their ever-jealous and greedy tormentors, it unfolds plainly as that.

In the context of this narrative, this adventure story as it were, the *Gita*'s spirit could easily be summarized into what in modern terms we might call a pep talk.

Don't be a chicken, cousin.

Gotta do what ya gotta do.

Fight the good fight. Fight for what is right.

In today's world, in today's world of work and life, the *Gita* appears remarkably close to nothing more than a coping philosophy[7].

> Contentment is all *Krishna* seems to be saying we must secure for ourselves; through discipline of thought, word, action, life, pleasure, duty.

Do what you can, don't stress what you can't control.

In critical academic terms, the *Gita*, of course, merely perpetuates what the critics have already said of Hinduism, a calculus of social oppression; "do caste-duty, kill".

But the *Gita* has to be more. Like most great strivings in culture, its alleged faults may be really reflections of our limitations in perception, rather than its inherent truth.

It has to be about finding the Greatest Love. The *Vishwaroopa Darshana* that Krishna gave to *Arjuna* was no psychedelic rock album cover art. Whatever happened, *Arjuna* felt it.

He forgot it later.

We would too, most likely.

But every moment must be for that only, for a glimpse of That. Again and again.

The greatest love.

Sometimes, the greatest of hates are the fields of action through we must be drawn, like the Pandavas' chariots, sometimes, in some relationships, like *Abhimanyu* perhaps, bound to destruction in the end.

For That, alone.

Till then, we cultivate yearning.

***

Yearning is good, learning is good, doing things selflessly is good.

Being content is of course even better. Being content, that is, without becoming complacent.

> It takes a great act of cultural detachment, ethical struggle, and spiritual will to say, *no, all of this is wrong.*

We must feel like we never *need* to act, that's how cool we must be. But we must act like the whole of life itself depends on it.

Longing without craving.

A vigilant contentment.

Contentment is all *Krishna* seems to be saying we must secure for ourselves; through discipline of thought, word, action, life, pleasure, duty, for the individual, and through the evolution of social order, work, governance, culture, law, everything, for everything beyond the individual.

But hasn't that been the Hindu problem of history?

That we have been keen to apply our famed philosophy to our individual success, and not to the greater social imagination? Is this sort of individualism a sort of freedom, a benign liberalism that lets us all chart our own courses, or is it merely an avoidance of something we have lacked a discourse for and about?

That we have been too much like *Krishna* told us to be; detached, content, shaking our heads this way and that way, saying yes-yes-yes and doing what we want because in the cosmic scheme of things nothing really matters?

That we have not yet found a voice for what it means to speak of a Hindu world today, or of the world as Hindus today?

***

Without a vision for the world in which we live today, *Krishna's* exhortation can become, in less skilled hands, mere technicism, a blind faith in technique, in method, in thinking only of how to get what we want rather than how to know what is good[8].

In post-liberalization India, it seems like that already. The ideal of *Satyameva Jayate* still stands in our lives, but in a perverted way[9]. After decades of corruption and venality, we have come to believe it not so much as 'truth always wins', but the opposite; 'whatever succeeds must be true'. If everyone is 'eating', as we say in India, then we must 'eat' too, that is the *dharma*. It takes a great act of cultural detachment, ethical struggle, and spiritual will to say, *no, all of this is wrong, corruption cannot be a way of life.*

In the global scale, technicism plays out more generally in the belief that might is right, in the myth about violence and nature, as we saw earlier in the book.

In post clash-of-civilizations America, already the high noon of everyday technicism, where meaning is polarized between cool *New Yorker* irony on one end of the political spectrum, and searing *Fox News* rage and literalism on the other, there might be a cold resonance to the *Gita's* seemingly impersonal code of action too.

You are not really killing anyone or anything, you are not doing anything, really, it's all playing out on its own anyway. It has become too easy to say that.

In the present American pop cultural climate of serial killer shows, autopsy festivals, torture porn movies, and general desecration of the integrity of the body in the name of art, entertainment, or individual freedom, it sounds like the sort of thing people are into now anyway.

You quote lines about Shiva, the Hollywood God of Death, as atom bombs go off[10]. You find Hindu detachment strangely

Maybe *Krishna* saw it all coming.
Maybe the real Kurukshetra is now before us.

appropriate to recognizing the impenetrable force of pure evil today; great destructiveness, great amoral systems of force and order.

Neither conventional religions with their eschatological promises of salvation, nor modern ideals of secular justice and progress with their promises of human rights and dignity seem capable of delivering, given the odds of what *extremes of delusion* this world runs on now.

Hinduism seems somehow above it all, and so much below it, under the radar of the present. We seem too much like a religion for the corporate soul now. The Hindu thing today seems to be: study hard, work hard, do your duty, don't stress about expectations and god will give you all the good things you need now, and that one great thing of release in the end, that *moksha* from the cycle of birth and death too if you are good; if your *karmic* account book balances, that is.

Hinduism is ever new, ever present. Hindu detachment can help us survive anything.

But is there a Hindu stand?

A Hindu line in the sand that says, till here, and only here, and no more?

A Hindu conch-shell blast to stop the world on its present course of self-destruction?

Maybe *Krishna* saw it all coming.

Maybe the real Kurukshetra is now before us.

***

We wake up, suddenly, from this dream that we have been in; this dream of being a son, brother, student, friend, party fiend, job-seeker, careerist, colleague, lover, romantic, spouse, parent, stranger, Facebook page, Twitter h@ndle, all of these things; we wake up and see a battle-field arrayed menacingly in front of us.

> You stand in history, in a chain of causes and effects, in this moment, and your Hinduism is now asking you to see it all, clearly.

It is not our relatives, our temptations, metaphors for anything.

It is not a flashback to a literal battle outside what is now Delhi five thousand years ago when *Krishna* and the *Pandavas* were really there, like you and me, fighting.

It is the present.

It is this planet, now. It is every crime against decency, dignity, life, and truth that is spread out before you[11].

It is inequality, injustice, and greed. It is the relentless destructiveness of its bulldozers, tanks, bombers, oil tankers, cargo ships, trains, cars, mine-shafts, power grids, slaughter-houses, factories, it is all there.

It is its mind chemistry of delusion and cruelty, in every twitching brain cell that turns husbands into abusers, children into punks, parents into tyrants, wives into terrors, friends into cheats, hands into instruments of death, tongues (and thumbs) into barbed wires whips of calumny and untruth.

It is this world, as it is now.

Mother Earth.

Brother Labour[12].

We have to see it clearly. But we are deluded, we only see illusions. We see burning light in hand-held gadgets and call it entertainment, reality, even life. We see things in shopping malls that we want but do not really need. We see brand names and price tags that we are defined by. We see things we want and cannot have and feel envious. We think that is what the fight is about; that we must fight office politics and our difficulties in facing them with sayings from the *Gita* and then simply get ahead in career and life. That is not unimportant, but that is not the only fight you are in now, and you must recognize that. You stand in history, in a chain of causes and effects, in this moment, and your Hinduism is now asking you to see it all, clearly.

But we see only distraction and pleasure, easily available, and chase them like predators and think it is here without cost, to us and to others.

We wake up, again, on a battlefield. It is the present. The battle is not over. Victory and peace were only dreams. We are back, at the beginning, again. Like a baby crying because it is about to forget all it knew as Truth before entering the bad dream of *samsara* all over again.

We wake up, again, in our suburban homes, in our apartments, in our office cubicles, in our anonymous cocoons in trains and planes, in these, our agri-business-raised bodies, our iEyes, in our school and media made minds, we blink.

We blink, and we wonder, why now? Why this? Why are we here in this place, at this time? What is this reality, what is all this, *really*?

We wake up to all this, and fearful, we ask.

We ask, are you here, O *Krishna*?

Are you?

***

We wake up, again, in our suburban homes, in our apartments, in our office cubicles, in our anonymous cocoons in trains and planes, in these, our agri-business-raised bodies, our iEyes, in our school and media made minds, we blink.

We blink, and we wonder, why now? Why this? Why are we here in this place, at this time? What is this reality, what is all this, really?

Our desire in rearming Hinduism is not to harm anybody, but only to disarm the ignorance that causes harm in this world.

Conclusion

JAGAT GURU[1]

When *Sanathana* Answers the Questions of *Desa* and *Kala*

Kasi.

May 2014.

Like a great whale rising, like *Matsya's* forehead shining in the dark night of an endless storm, a mighty civilization is finding itself once again.

It is bound to cause a splash. It is a whale, a primordial living giant. But it is not like a tree falling. It is therefore a symbol of life rather than death.

It is playing.

It is time though to stop counting the drops and start getting ready for the journey itself. What I mean by that is that the present moment is not just about one country being taken back by its people.

A reborn Hinduism is a promise reborn for all this world too.

It is not just a civilization rising, but Civilization itself.

In our ship story, we take everybody, and everything with us.

We believe in just One thing.

We don't differentiate, but having been forced into the language of difference, we will now assume the place we have to for now, one among civilizations as others may see it, one among powers as others may call it, but our purpose is not to simply turn into another nationalist fantasy about world domination.

Our desire in rearming Hinduism is not to harm anybody, but only to disarm the ignorance that causes harm in this world, wherever it may be.

Our desire in rearming Hinduism is not to deny anybody, but to do what must be done to secure the conditions that will give everybody freedom; freedom from hurt and harm, most of all; the conditions that will give them peace, justice, prosperity.

Our desire is to teach ourselves first, and then teach others too.

Our destiny is to let life know itself again.

We have *desa* and *kala* on our side again. *Sanathana* is waiting. The morning rays fall on the face of *Vishnu* as He begins His day all over again.

***

It is not an exaggeration to say that the hope that 2014 has brought to many in India marks one of the most important and inspiring turning-points in the history of not just India but the world too.

It marks not only the restoration of an honored place for Hindu civilization in the land of its birth, or India's pride in world affairs, but something even more important and crucial: 2014 marks the return of intelligence as a guiding force over human destiny.

When Hinduphobia is removed from historiography as we have begun to do in this book, we will understand the story of the world much more accurately.

That has been India's role historically in the course of the world. Others may have imparted to the world their contributions, their intelligence manifest as inventions and technology, but that kind of intelligence has often come at an enormous cost to the planet and its life. The rise of Europe marked that phase. The relative decline of that dominance, and the imminent restoration of the ancient civilizations of the earth, rooted in a far more universal, ecological and ethical sense of intelligence, will end the Icarian hurtle that modern civilization is presently facing. In the last 500 years, we have learned to fly, truly, and having flown too close to the sun, we must now know again that we are the children of this earth and not its masters.

When Hinduphobia is removed from historiography as we have begun to do in this book, we will understand the story of the world much more accurately. The story of the world we have been taught in the last few centuries, virtually anywhere on earth is the same. It is Eurocentric, anthropocentric, and contains biases and distortions so deep most of them are yet to be named. Less than one hundred years after European colonialism ended, and almost exactly one hundred years after the invention of mass industrial warfare, we must confront the pure evil that this model of 'humanity' bequeathed by colonialism's one-eyed vision[2] of things has left us with. At the peak of their power, a small group of nations held their dominance like a jackboot on the lives of the whole planet, smashing over whatever good sense might have held their predation in check. They might have been able to do it because their (mis)use of intelligence was rewarding in material terms, in the short-term. They had guns, germs and steel on their side, we are told. But what they were guided by was not intelligence in the way we understand it. It was only power.

All of social science and history, and even the discussion on religion and civilization today, is rooted in the singular worship of power. It was the definitive characteristic of the colonizer's view of life, the view we have all inherited now. It was not enough for the colonialists to plunder, rule, enslave, and convert; the most telling moment of their identity-performance was the *shikhar*. It was in the extermination of nature's greatest symbols of power, the tiger, the lion, and most of all the great *Ganesha* himself, the elephant, that their power-thirst was, somewhat, sated. It was a dangerous sort of power-trip. It began with destructiveness. Why it was like that, we might come to know only when better historiographies emerge, when monsoon-determinism is replaced in scholarship perhaps with some overdue attention to the ice-age.

Having said that, we must also recognize that the era of European colonialism established one thing that might well prove to be the foundation for a better, or at least, a slightly less-destructive way of living in the near future. Confronted by power, and violent, destructive power at that (and we must acknowledge that the European nations were not alone at that time in history in the use of violent force for conquest, nor pseudo-religious ideology as a justification for it), European colonialism set in place for the first time universalism as a universal, or at least a global social reality. One story, one set of laws, one sense of humanity. Of course, it took many centuries of fighting racism to make universalism truly universal; or at least challenge the hierarchies of race, gender, and most of all, species. The present challenge in academics is of course to rise above the near total dissolution of the promise of universalism into the superficially empowering language of postmodern relativism and identity politics.

In India, both these phases have ended.

May 1998 was India's statement that it possessed the language that colonialism had stipulated as the one you had to speak if you were not to be ignored, rendered invisible, that is. It was India's statement in the language of *power* established by colonial universalism.

But we have also now witnessed May 2014.

We are the custodians and children of this moment.

We are *Saraswathi's* children, first.

May 2014 is India's statement that another language is not just possible, but inevitable; it is the language of intelligence, of universal kindness, of civilization.

***

Satya and *Maya* have never before been so clearly polarized in recent times as they have during the 2014 elections. The language of *maya* is powerful, persistent; it has the backing of sixty-six years of postcolonial privilege in India, and five hundred years of colonial support; it is the language of the powerful, even if it speaks about empowering the powerless and protecting minorities and such. It has become so deceitful, that it has been rejected, even if those who have rejected it risk the stigma of being labeled as fascists, dictators, haters, and worse. Our kindness must be strong, and in the end stronger than their delusions.

We who believe in the promise of this moment in history must now strive towards embodying our hopes in realities. What we have won now is not merely a chance for India to catch up with illusions of progress as defined by those who do not know better, but the opportunity to assert *Satya*, truth itself, over an age defined by the illusions of mass media. We must respect what has given us this gift, what has given us our culture and civilization too, and that is intelligence. We are *Saraswathi's* children, first. Our wisdom will bring *Lakshmi*, and all else too, but we need them together. One without the other is never sustainable.

A civilization of intelligence is speaking as it should. We dream of making India great once again, but not in the clichéd and insincere ways we have heard in the past. We cannot make India great by

> The greatest hunger today in our young is not just for wealth and success, but increasingly for purpose and meaning too.

promising to send men to the moon to please the middle-class and promising hand-outs to others and ultimately doing neither well. We are now talking about the reality that confronts us every day. We will clean our streets before we put up space stations. We will feed our poor before we build abandoned stadia. Most of all, we will give ourselves a hope based in truth and dignity once again.

The light of India shines not in its mineral deposits or its medal-tallies at the Olympics. It is in every pair of eyes you see in its land.

***

It takes intelligence, more than anything else, to choose life over destruction, kindness over cruelty, and love over hate. It takes intelligence, first of all, to know truth over delusion, to know what is life, and what is the Matrix; to know most of all, what is kindness, and what is cruelty.

It takes intelligence to know that in the well-being of all lies the well-being of one too.

It takes intelligence to know that love is inevitable.

***

For several decades, if not centuries now, our intelligence has been distracted. Forced by circumstances not mostly of our own making, we have reduced our intelligence to the terms set by others, to the single-minded pursuit of skills, jobs, and money. These are not unimportant. Our survival depended on it, and still does. But in the urgency of surviving colonialism, and then a highly elitist half a century of postcolonial self-neglect, we very nearly forgot who we really are.

Now we have remembered. We are awake. And we must get to work.

The greatest hunger today in our young is not just for wealth and success, but increasingly for purpose and meaning too. We know, in our hearts, that much of what we have been told about ourselves by the illusions of Hinduphobia are false, and we have held on still, sometimes blindly, sometimes even at the cost of being ridiculed, to our gods and our gurus. We have faced, for at least a few decades now, the disconnect between our inner world of belief, of our gods and their lives, and the world of the present and the future. When we tried to make the two speak to each other, we were often dismissed as fundamentalists. We were not successful because we did not yet have the intellectual resources to do so, we did not have our vision for our nation fully restored. We did what we could do, under the circumstances, and when our frustration could no longer be contained, we used the language of the times to express it, lashing out at people and communities, though it was not our first choice to do so at all.

We now have the chance to do more than react. We have the chance to lead ourselves, which is as important, as leading the world.

***

This, we can accomplish in our lifetimes.

We can change the course of social investment, in India, and then, by speaking universally — for universalism comes naturally to us — in all of the world too. We cannot have a world in which the dominant way of life is based on sheer, steely violence for much

---

> We cannot have a world in which the dominant way of life is based on sheer, steely violence for much longer.

> We are living in the most extreme stages of a moral and civilizational failure of monstrous proportions.

longer. We must teach ourselves, and the world, to first recognize that the present course of history is unnatural, unsustainable, and unjust. We must learn to respect life, again.

One plan of action can be inferred from our own past. If we reject the Hinduphobic account of Hindu history as a process of invasion and gradual civilization from a violent Vedic past to its present fundamentalist future, if we step beyond the limitations of seeing our scriptures as nothing more than reflections of politics between social groups, if we see the philosophy of devotion in them, then we can recognize a more meaningful narrative at once historic and spiritual.

We begin with *Tvameva*, the love that makes us see the other as our own, the love that is one without a second. Our oldest scriptures teach us that, and in each of our lives too, we begin that way.

We then move towards relationships, *bandhu* and *sakha*, the challenge of finding love and kindness and justice in our relationships with others, in our families, and at the larger social, national and global levels. Our epics express that complexity, not because they want to oppress people, but because they want to show us that this too has happened, this too will pass, this too will have to fall before love.

Or, to put is more simply:

The *Vedas* said God is One, Everything is One.

Then, the *Upanishads* said since it's all one, don't be selfish.

Then, the *Puranas* said, since life is complicated, and it is not easy to be unselfish, learn to be in *dharma*, and spelled that out in the *Gita*.

We have been living in this world ever since, ever new.

***

The history of human civilization, contrary to some current myths, is marked by an increasing dependence on the centrality of violence. In the past few centuries, with the rise of colonial modernity and in the aftermath of postcolonial modernity in which our lives unfold now, the mediation of society by violence has only increased. Simply put, each of our bodies, whether we are personally violent or not, now consume resources extracted by a worldwide system of violence, against people, animals, fish, birds, and even trees. The birth of a child in the middle or upper classes anywhere on earth marks the end of the lives of so many living beings, whether we realize it or not (and as if trees are not enough, there is now a proposal to kill jelly-fish to make diapers, believe it or not, and those jelly-fish[3] apparently are proliferating because almost all the other fish in the oceans have been factory-farmed!). For five hundred years, we have covered up a way of life based on killing with niceties and promises like human rights. We are living in the most extreme stages of a moral and civilizational failure of monstrous proportions.

But the future, and the promises given to us by millions of years of evolution can still be changed and they will be changed if you decide that this is what you must do with your life, now. That is Hinduism's greatest gift to humanity. Our ancestors did not merely 'survive' in the sense of fighting and killing the weak. They worshipped and cultivated intelligence steeped in kindness; for each human being, it meant a promise of the greatest fulfillment. For society, it meant administering the use of force wisely, with the least harm possible. Now, we must once again channel our social investment in a way that does the greatest good for all, which also means the *least harm for all*.

We may not be able to remove violence from our world, but we can minimize it, and we can reduce our dependence on it.

We may not be able to remove violence from our world, but we can minimize it, and we can reduce our dependence on it.

***

Five is an auspicious number in our culture. Five elements, five senses, five-faced depictions for our deities. Five can inform our understanding of history, of our place in time, in a unique way as well. Like the *Pancha-mukha Anjaneya*, seeing with five faces, we might recognize now that each of one of us goes through our lifespans essentially interacting with no more than five streams in time, five generations. For most human beings, their lifespans allow an interaction with their grandparents, their parents, their own generation, their children, and then perhaps their grandchildren.

Five generations, each overlapping, can be a powerful force for changing the course of history, if we want it.

If you are young, think of the world and its circumstances when your parents were young, and their parents. Think of what has changed, for the better, and for worse. How much more or less did each generation consume? What is your generation doing? What will you do when you are older?

School and college do not prepare us for life's choices like friendship, marriage, family, love, peace, moral choices, much less for destiny and history. We must think for ourselves about what is to be achieved and how to do so. Sometimes, the smallest actions count; turning off your chat session, putting down the remote, putting one less piece of junk food into your body, and simply, breathing, laughing, and maybe, smiling at someone.

If you are older, a parent or a grandparent, perhaps, compare the worlds in change that you see. You are probably striving to give your children a better life than you did, in material terms and perhaps in other ways too. You must recognize one thing though. Our time in history, as the last children of Nehru's India (or Gandhi's India, if

> Secularization was a response to a time and place in history when science was young and needed protection from superstition.

you are a grandparent), gave us some gifts, but also left us in limbo as far as a true education in our past and present was concerned. We are only now beginning to connect the dots between them, between our civilization and the future of the world. We must cultivate our sensibility now.

For that we need knowledge, social knowledge. We need to know why and how our assumptions about reality, about history, not just of India or Hinduism, but of humanity and nature itself, have been shaped the way they have. Knowledge, in Indian thought, does not believe in the separation of the spiritual and the material. Yet, in the modern world, we have lived with our hearts and feet in both, inadequately. So far, at least. What we can find now is something that has rarely been done before. We must direct our social investment into the rediscovery of our civilization and philosophy, and ensure the conditions needed to make it inform our shared future. In our own lives too, in each of our lives, amidst our own relations, obligations, loves and losses, we must find that dialogue between the material and the spiritual. We must move beyond God as our go-to miracle-dispenser, and cultivate a sense of wonder about the mysteries of this living world (and this lived-in world), and most of all, let it speak to our sense of purpose, destiny, and moral empowerment. We must learn to recognize, most of all, that God, at least in Hindu thought, is not some far off creator, but a deeply intimate, human, and social player. We walk a fine line perfected over millennia in our comprehension of the divine. We will walk some more.

You might be spiritual and not religious. You might be both. You might be secular. You might be an atheist. You might be a

> The history that created the present is only this: a time and place steeped in violence collided into Hinduism five hundred years ago, and the first truly world civilization was born.

cultural Hindu rather than a religious one. Whoever you are now, and whoever you want to be, in your life is a legacy of great lives unfolding even now, their wisdom, their art, and most of all, their love for all of life itself. If any of this moves you, if anything makes you feel, if your gods, their images, their stories, all of these stir your heart in ways that you cannot explain, then you are now well on board for the next great journey in human redemption. We have already entered a moment in modern life when the old disdain for the spirit is rapidly eroding. Secularization was a response to a time and place in history when science was young and needed protection from superstition. But hopefully, as this book might have indicated, there is far more to Hinduism and the rediscovery of Hindu thought and culture than personal, individual stress-busting, or fascistic social oppression. Understood a little better, the intellectual journey of our ancestors from a simple statement of the self's surrender to the Other to complex assertions of love and duty, can lead us to a better world. In today's science-centered culture we are beginning to recognize spirituality too, although mostly in medical terms. The spiritual, in a way, has been contained, rendered apolitical and unprogressive, by being reduced to medicine and therapy; but once it touches the domain of our popular story about ourselves, once we reexamine our commonsense in the social sciences, we will achieve something the scholars and activists who work in these fields have been trying to do a lot better as well.

The past few centuries have seen the quiet erasure of Hinduism from official history, from the commonsense story of the world and of our selves we carry around all our lives. We have seen our numerals become Arabic numerals and then European numerals and universal symbols. We have seen our ideas and contributions diffuse so much into the human quest that we do not even recognize our own any more. One day, perhaps, scholars with honesty will inquire and will find that much of the modern world we live in today, with its promises of freedom, equality, justice, democracy, all of this have somehow emerged in that great encounter between India and the West which was the bedrock of today's global society. From many centres of perception in the world arose one. We are beginning to unravel its blindness now. We can see our yoga save bodies, and maybe spirits too, even if some of its beneficiaries wish to obfuscate its origins and philosophies. We can see our ancient sensibilities watered down now as secularism. We see our most cherished ideals like *satya*, as universalism now, and *ahimsa*, as the discourse of human rights, and the still nascent language of animal rights. The history that created the present is only this: a time and place steeped in violence collided into Hinduism five hundred years ago, and the first truly world civilization was born. We Hindus endured it somehow, as it grew on the backs of our labourers, our scientists, our teachers, and on the prosperity we once had with our peppers and spices. We might have been conquered, but we were never defeated. We retreated, strategically, for a few generations, so the *sanathana dharma* could learn the customs of this new *desa* and *kala*, this modern world. Now that we have learned, we will teach again. We learn after all, from nothing less than this universe itself.

We asked who we are.

Krishna has answered.

Jagat Guru.

***

Samastha Jeeva Sukhino Bhavanthu
Om Shanti Shanti Shanti

***

We might have been conquered, but we were never defeated. We retreated, strategically, for a few generations, so the *sanathana dharma* could learn the customs of this new *desa* and *kala,* this modern world. Now that we have learned, we will teach again.

NOTES

Preface: Your Hinduism

1. *"Gayatri Mantra"*
As this is not a textbook or user-manual, translations are evocative rather than literal.

2. *"Sanskriti"*
Excerpts below from the group email sent out to members of the Sanskriti email list (passed on to me by an alum) on January 27, 2009 summarizing arguments:

"FOR the name change:

1. The term "Sanskriti" has certain associations with the Hindu fundamentalist movement, both in South Asia and the United States. The discourse of Sanskriti has been widely used in a discriminatory, communalist fashion to incite hatred and Hindu nationalism.

2. The term "Sanskriti" has its root in Sanskrit (and a few related languages), Hinduism, and primarily north India. Thus, it can be an alienating term to people from other parts of South Asia.

AGAINST the name change:

1. The term may be used independently of Hindu fundamentalism and should be reclaimed from the Hindu right-wing.

2. Some people may not feel alienated by the term…"

3. *"Economist" "Onion"*
The Economist (July 21, 2011). Fleeting Chance.

The Onion (September 13, 2012). No one murdered because of this image.

4. *"Wendy Doniger…."*
For a specific example of Doniger's response to the controversy see her op-ed:

Wendy Doniger (March 6, 2014). Banned in Bangalore. *The New York Times*.

Also see:

Vamsee Juluri & Murali Balaji (2014). 50 Shades of Mayo: Cultural Imperialism, Orientalism and the Media Framing of an Indian Book Battle. Paper presented at the *International Association of Media and Communication Research (IAMCR) Conference*, Hyderabad, India.

5. *"Vedic Hindus… Cowboys and Nazis.."*
See p. 111 and p. 144 of *The Hindus: An Alternative History*.

6 *"State of Religion Atlas"*
According to this otherwise authoritative-sounding book, Hinduism is India's "state religion established in law" (56-57).
Joanne O'Brien and Martin Palmer (1993). *The State of Religion Atlas*. New York: Simon and Schuster.

7 *"…. several op-ed pieces that blame India's policy on Kashmir, the rise of 'Hindu extremism,' and the appalling state of poverty among Muslims in India"*
Amitav Ghosh (December 3, 2008). India's 9/11? Not Exactly. *The New York Times.*
Arundhati Roy (December 12, 2008) 9 is not 11. *The Huffington Post.*
Asra Nomani (December 1, 2008). Muslims: India's New Untouchables. *The Los Angeles Times.*
Martha Nussbaum (November 30, 2008) A Cloud Over India's Muslims. *The Los Angeles Times.*
Pankaj Mishra (December 1, 2008). Fresh Blood from an Old Wound. *New York Times.*
Suketu Mehta (November 29, 2008). What they Hate about Mumbai. *The New York Times.*
Also see my discussion of these articles:
Vamsee Juluri (December 17, 2008). How the West Lost Us: A Critique of the Media Coverage of the Mumbai Attacks. *The Hoot/ The Huffington Post/ Asia Pacific Perspectives Journal.*

8. *"Gujarat…"*
See Arundhati Roy's article, including the much repeated quote about "fetuses ripped from mothers' wombs":

Arundhati Roy (May 6, 2002). Democracy: Who is she when she is at home? *Outlook.*

Also see the refutation:

Balbir Punj (May 27, 2002). Fiddling with Facts as Gujarat Burns. *Outlook*.

The story about German soldiers bayoneting babies in the first world war is a well known example in the history of propaganda; this myth also reappeared in the Western press coverage of Saddam Hussain's invasion of Kuwait in the form of an allegation that Iraqi soldiers had thrown out Kuwaiti babies from their incubators, a charge that reportedly led to widespread American support for the war. For more see:

Brooke Gladstone & Josh Neufield (2011). *The Influencing Machine*. New York: Norton

9. *"Mama dehi karaavalambam"*
Sri Sankaracharya, Lakshmi-Narasimha Stotram.

Chapter 1. The Academic Mayasabha

1. *"… how blind academia is today to its most pernicious prejudice"*
Jakob de Roover (2014 March). Untangling the knot. *Outlook*.

Lisa Lau and Ana Mendes (eds). (2011). *Reorientalism and South Asian Identity Politics: The Oriental Other Within*. New York: Routledge

Krishnan Ramaswamy, Antonio de Nicolas & Aditi Banerjee (eds.). (2007). *Invading the Sacred: An Analysis of Hinduism Studies in America*. New Delhi: Rupa.

2. *"There is really no religion called Hinduism; it was invented by the British and the Brahmins only in the 19th century."*
Along with the paradoxical claim that Hindus conquered India from outside, this view seems to the current orthodoxy in parts of academia and journalism. For an example see:

Pankaj Mishra (2009 April 24) Another incarnation (Review of *The Hindus: An Alternative History*). *New York Times*.

3. *"A note on objectivity, method… social sciences"*
The book "Truth" in the Keywords series is useful, especially Daniel Patterson's chapter on what he calls "American classroom relativism," and also Ganesh Devy on truth in Indian traditions, including the Upanishads, Natya Shastra, bhakti literature, and Hind Swaraj.

Nadia Tazi (ed.). (2004). *Keywords: Truth*. New Delhi: Vistaar.

Also watch the documentary The First Measured Century for fascinating examples of early 20th century pseudo-social science.

http://www.pbs.org/fmc/

For an engaging critique of the rise of the Western academy's "idea of India" see:

Ronald Inden (1990). *Imagining India*. Bloomington: Indiana University.

The connection between 19th century European missionary biases, racial theory, and the emerging field of European writing on Hinduism, is examined in the early chapters of Rajiv Malhotra and Aravindan Neelakandan's book *Breaking India*.

Rajiv Malhotra and Aravindan Neelakandan (2011). *Breaking India: Interventions in Dravidian and Dalit Faultlines*. New Delhi: Amaryllis.

4. *"Kennedy once told Nehru…"*
Andrew Rotter (2000). *Comrades at Odds: The United States and India, 1947-1964*. Ithaca: Cornell University Press.

5. *"Orientalism is a discourse"*
Edward Said (1978). *Orientalism*. New York: Vintage.

6. *"American cold war calculations…"*
Andrew Rotter identifies monotheism, diet, and the image of a martial race as some of the things that Washington saw as shared cultural traits with Islamabad in the 1950s.

7. *"The Hindu in today's academic and pop culture stereotype…"*
A well-known case of media stereotyping was the decision of the makers of the hit 2008 movie *Slumdog Millionaire* to change the identity of the protagonist from that of a religious everyman in the novel to a Muslim oppressed by Hindus. A poor Muslim is also the protagonist in Katherine Boo's acclaimed *Behind the Beautiful Forevers*. In addition to this rather simplified understanding of Hindu as rich/oppressive, there is also a constant distortion in the discourse around the bogey of Hindu nationalism. Hindu nationalism may be a real phenomenon, but it is rarely addressed in the context of the many identity-based political movements (and militancies) that arose in India since the 1980s. Instead, any

discussion on Hinduism today seems to be singularly obsessed with an over-imagined "Hindu nationalist" foe. It appears very few academicians actually address Hindus or students of Hinduism in their writing today, preferring to argue with a strawman (which might be drawn, sometimes, like in the book *Hinduism for Beginners*, as a strongman). Some day we may wake up and realize this whole discourse was as absurd and calculated as the question "have you stopped beating your wife?"

Chapter 2. The Myth of an Alternative History

1. *"Howard Zinn…"*
Howard Zinn (1980). *A People's History of the United States: 1492 to the Present*. New York: Harper.

2. *"Sen, Nussbaum, …"*
See my e-single essay *Hinduism and its Culture Wars* for more on this. The discourse on India and Hinduism today in America is defined almost exclusively by this small group of writers — who seemingly lack an interest or insight into how Hinduism is lived. Sen, for example, mentions in *The Argumentative Indian* that he grew up in a house without religious rituals, an unusual situation in India (p. 45).

Amartya Sen (2005). *The Argumentative Indian: Writings on Indian History, Culture and Identity*. New York: Farrar, Straus and Giroux.

Martha Nussbaum (2007). *The Clash Within: Democracy, Religious Violence and India's Future*. Cambridge: Harvard University.

Vamsee Juluri (2014). *Hinduism and its Culture Wars: How Secularism Lost its Way to Hinduphobia*. Tranquebar Press (e-single).

3 *"British-intellectual class…"*
Perry Anderson (2012 July 5). Gandhi Centre Stage. London Review of Books.

4. *"…religion critic Sam Harris…"*
Sam Harris (2005). *The End of Faith: Religion, Terror and Faith*. New York: Norton

5. *"We ethnics are all ruled by our cultures…"*
This is a widespread trope in American commonsense, a manifestation perhaps of mythologies of American exceptionalism, individualism and

freedom. James Carey discusses this in his classic essay Communication and Culture; the belief is that while Americans are free, others tend to be determined by their religion or culture. An especially comical example of this used to appear in the landscape of 1990s TV wrestling. A vaguely "oriental" wrestler character used to go around on the show growling something like "you een-sult my culture, I keell you!"

James Carey (1989). *A Cultural Approach to Communication*. New York: Routledge.

6. *"Caste…"*

The caste critique of Hindu history is an important one and I do not equate it morally or politically with what I view as Hinduphobia. The intellectual challenge of the moment is to be able to recognize the realities of caste identities and politics beyond Hinduphobic generalizations and inaccuracies. One challenge is specific to the nature of the institutional location of much Hinduphobic discourse in the Western media and academy, where the discourse and the commonsense lack a nuanced understanding of the whole spectrum of political change in India. Not unlike Carey's point above, we find that the word "caste" becomes in American conversation the sole determinant of every Hindu's thought, word and action, and often erroneously. Like the story about the American audience applauding the maestro Ravi Shankar and his musicians for just tuning their instruments (the 1971 Concert for Bangladesh), today's enlightened Western observer perhaps mistakenly sees caste determination in actions even where there isn't any. The perception of caste as an eternal, unchanging essence in India (and as the definitive feature of Hinduism) needs some updates from reality; whether that is Sanskritization, Mandalization, or just the fact that caste has retained its form in India outside Hinduism too.

Interestingly, even Doniger acknowledges that caste was not the unchanging hierarchy it is assumed to be in Indian history and that communities as a whole could move up the caste ladder (p 286). Presumably, an insight as important as this would inform the rest of the argument, but it really doesn't.

The equation of class and caste in simplified terms remains as it has in academia and popular culture. On a PBS travel show about a Western spiritual seeker's travel to India to meet the Dalai Lama, the narrator describes the wealthy members of a polo club he visits as unhappy

"Brahmins." The assumption that the "highest" caste must be the wealthiest one runs deep, and new political realities, such as the poverty among Brahmins, or the alliance of Dalits and Brahmins in parts of India are seldom recognized as well. Doniger also cites an excerpt from the Manu Smriti about punishments for caste violations (p. 304). While the thoughts expressed in this excerpt are deplorable, the question also remains if such punishments are indeed a reality today, or does reproducing them (as the movie *Bandit Queen* does, with the Tulasidas quote about donkeys, women and lower castes) perpetuate a myth about modern Hindus as tyrannical fundamentalists outside the pale of civilization and India's constitution.

7. *"We go in to study the Ramayana and Mahabharatha on TV, or how Amar Chitra Kathas are read"*

The rise of Hindutva is one of the most frequently researched topics in media and cultural studies. Numerous studies of the Ramayan and Mahabharath TV series of the 1980s have explored the connection between these serials and the rise of Hindutva. Mankekar and Rajagopal's studies are particularly insightful. The problem, however, is that the field has not moved beyond studies that examine religion as a political identity and taken up questions of what religion means to people. Rachel Dwyer makes this point in her study *Filming the Gods*.

Purnima Mankekar (1999). *Screening Culture, Viewing Politics: An Ethnography of Television, Womanhood and Nation in Postcolonial India.* Durham: Duke.

Arvind Rajagopal (2001). *Politics after Television. Hindu nationalism and the Reshaping of the Public in India.* Cambridge: Cambridge University.

Katherine McClain (2009). *India's Immortal Comic Books: Gods, Kings and Other Heroes.* Bloomington: Indiana University.

Rachel Dwyer (2006). *Filming the Gods: Religion in Indian Cinema.* New York: Routledge.

Chapter 3. The Myth of Aryan Origins

1 *"California history textbooks"*

WMDs all over again. In early 2006, Hindu American parents in California sought changes in the content of their children's school textbooks, a request that had been routinely granted to various minority communities to ensure accuracy and end past racial prejudices and stereotypes. The

Hinduism lessons contained questionable colonial-era assumptions about Hinduism's past such as the Aryan invasion theory and a mocking dismissive tone towards revered sacred figures like Hanuman. A large group of academics and activists misread this legitimate grievance. Romila Thapar and Michael Witzel argued this was an RSS plan to rewrite history (though Thapar has elsewhere expressed doubts about the Aryan invasion idea). I opposed this interpretation.

Romila Thapar & Michael Witzel (March 2006). A different agenda. *San Francisco Chronicle.*

Vamsee Juluri (March 2006). State textbooks contribute to ignorance about Hinduism. *San Francisco Chronicle.*

2. *"Eurocentrism ... ethnocentrism given an army, navy, media and universities to go global and universal with."*
Paraphrasing Samir Amin's memorable phrase.

Samir Amin (1978) *Eurocentrism*. New York: Monthly Review Press.

3. *"...Nazi policy of annexation"*
Doniger, *The Hindus*, p. 144.

4. *"...necrophilia, and it has been blamed, rightly in my view, for the vast destructiveness of modernity"*
Mahatma Gandhi's critique of violence and modernity, in my view, remains the most important, vital, and useful intellectual argument for changing today's world. Unfortunately, the substance of his thought is often ignored by critics of the Left and Right eager to dismiss the politics around his symbolism and his memory. I urge readers who feel a sense of betrayal about Gandhi's actions, whether about Partition or about the Poona Pact (though I understand that the Hindu grievance at Gandhi is different from the Dalit position) to hold those feelings aside and study *Hind Swaraj* at face-value for its powerful and global critique of a world (and worldview) going wrong.

Another key point to note is that Gandhian scholars have often pointed out that ahimsa is not merely pacifism or "turning the other cheek" as we understand it in layman's terms, but really an intellectual tradition, a method of critique. At the risk of simplifying, I would suggest that just as feminism helps us recognize patriarchy, and Marxism, issues of class, non-violence can be seen as a way for us to *recognize* violence in the world today, in "thought, word and deed," as Gandhi might say (or at the very least contest its normalization, as critical scholars might put it). Bhikhu Parekh's *Gandhi: A Very Short Introduction* is a concise and masterful introduction to this question. Ashis Nandy's essay, *Outside the Imperium,* also discusses some of these questions with great astuteness.

From a very different approach, the notion of "necrophilia" as discussed in the psychoanalyst Erich Fromm's work may also be useful to the growth of a vocabulary of critique for what ails the modern world's perception. For one thing, the last two decades have seen an astounding increase in what can only be described as necrophilia (in a voyeuristic, if not sexual sense as such) in the landscape of popular culture. The popular travelling exhibit Bodies, which displays mummified and partly dissected human cadavers, and the enormous attention to graphic depictions of death, decay, and mutilation in shows like CSI, constitute more than a passing fancy.

Bhikhu Parekh (1997) *Gandhi: A Very Short Introduction*. New York: Oxford University Press.

Ashis Nandy (1987). *From Outside the Imperium: Gandhi's Cultural Critique of the West*. In A. Nandy, *Traditions, Tyrannies and Utopias: Essays in the Politics of Awareness* (pp. 127-162). New Delhi: Oxford University Press.

Erich Fromm (1973). *The Anatomy of Human Destructiveness*. New York: Holt, Rhinehart & Wilston.

5. *"Richard Dawkins, a scientist-atheist in a long crusade"*
Dawkins has a problem with "origin myths" and with saying a "living creature" existed outside of physical reality before it began (p. 163). First of all, I doubt we would think of any of our gods as "living creatures" in the ordinary sense. Moreover, the way in which "origin myths" are expressed, lived, and understood in Hinduism today is probably very different from the way the modern, scientific mind talks about them. We don't think of Vishnu, say, when someone asks us "how did the world begin" but only when we need assurance or comfort in our daily lives. These are two separate spheres of existence and meaning. Science is well accepted in the Indian public sphere. As long as there is no coercion to replace it with the so called "origin myths," and *in India, there really hasn't been any,* the right of the devout to their own personal meanings should be respected

too. There needs to be a distinction made by atheist crusaders against the abuse of religious myth in legal and cultural wars against science and the popular and devotional evocation of gods and goddesses in peoples' lives. By the way, Dawkin's illustrator seems to think that *Vishnu*'s serpent is an angry one, fangs and all! We notice subtleties in our depictions that other presumably don't care to respect. *Adi Sesha* is eternity itself, and is peaceful and content in whatever depictions we have seen of him in art and sculpture. Sensibilities are important, and crassly ignoring them can be unscientific too (lay observers, like my former American landlady who balked at the *Adi Sesha* on the cover of my first book associating it in her mind with the serpent of Eden, can be excused!)

Richard Dawkins (2011) *The Magic of Reality: How We Know What's Really True*. New York: Free Press.

6. *"Hinduism is biocentric."*
S. Cromwell Crawford (2003). *Hindu Bioethics for the Twenty First Century*. Albany: SUNY.

7. *"Scientific theories and popular culture myths about prehistory and the origins of mankind...."*
Leakey points out these connections in a crisp summary, from Darwin's own times to the present; in the 1940s, when industry and inventiveness were the ideals of human progress, the key image in evolutionary discourse was "Man the Toolmaker." After the war, it was "Man the Killer Ape," and then "Man the Hunter." With the rise of women's studies in the 1970s, it became "Woman the Gatherer."

Richard Leakey (1994). *The Origin of Humankind*. New York: Harper.

8. *"... stories about cavemen, hunter-gatherers, monkeys"*
See:

Richard Bulliet (2005). *Hunters, Herders and Hamburgers: The Past and Future of Human-Animal Relationships*. New York: Columbia University.

Matt Cartmill (1993). *A View to a Death in the Morning: Hunting and Nature through History*. Cambridge: Harvard University.

9. *"... social functionalism."*
The reduction of god-stories or mythology by both Left and Right in a functionalist manner is a case in point. Critics of Hinduism tend to view stories about Rama and Krishna, for example, as code for social

oppression, and tools for domination to this day. Believers and supporters too, lacking an adequate vocabulary for expressing their meanings, turn to a simplistic functionalistic framework to try and explain their beliefs, appearing too defensive sometimes. A better way would be to acknowledge what these stories mean to the people who cherish them at face value, as "God stories," rather than as derivatives of something else.

Chapter 4. The Myth of Vedic Violence

1. *"the Vedas were also about killing and eating cows."*
D.N. Jha's The Myth of the Holy Cow is, fascinatingly enough, reviewed very positively in both very liberal and very conservative publications in the West. An example, perhaps, of my point earlier that the only thing the Left and Right in the US agree upon is their low view of Hinduism.

2. *"… ritual violence … social violence."*
Doniger, The Hindus, p. 103

3. *"Inaccuracies, distortions"*
For a critique of Doniger's book by a lay Hindu reader, see:

Vishal Agarwal (February 20, 2014). A Critique of Wendy Doniger's The Hindus: An Alternative History. *Hindureview.com*

Also see:

Nicholas O' Connell (2013). Freudian Psychoanalysis vs. Intellectual Rigor in Hinduism Studies. *Videshisutra.com*

http://videshisutra.com/2013/04/09/freudian-psychoanalysis-vs-intellectual-rigor-in-hinduism-studies/

4. *"… presume universality based upon their own past practices of violence."*
The assumption that violence has been as central to all ways of life and thought as its own is somewhat of an unexamined Eurocentric assumption. It may be true that no group of people has been entirely free of violence, but it does not mean everyone thinks the same way about the naturalness of violence, or resorts to it with the same ease that Eurocentric myths make it out to be. This assumption runs across the entire realm of thought today; from sophisticated academic theories to simple commonsense beliefs. For example, even a common gesture like the handshake is interpreted in popular websites as an ancient gesture

to show that one is not bearing weapons – rather than acknowledge that touch is simply a gesture of affection for living beings.

5. *"...its intellectual toolbox is yet to evolve a suitable critique of violence itself."*

My thinking on this question comes from my study of Gandhian scholarship. I turned to Gandhi while teaching a class called Media, Stereotyping and Violence several years ago, shortly after the 9/11 terror attacks. My students had specific questions about violence and human nature. In class discussions, we often found most of us agreeing with the statement "human nature is violent". But on closer scrutiny, we could see how this was a belief naturalized by certain narratives in the popular culture. Gandhi's saying that "history as we know it is a record of the wars of the world" is instructive here: we write history in terms of battles and deaths not because everything that happened was violent, but because those violent events were *interruptions* to "the course of nature."

Juluri (2004). Violence and Nonviolence in Media Studies. *Communication Theory*, 15, 2, pp. 196-215.

Juluri (2006). Media Wars in Gandhian Perspective. *Peace Review. A Journal of Social Justice*, 17, 4, pp. 397–402.

6. *"the sun wouldn't rise..."*

We might grant that the phrase about the sun is perhaps used casually by Doniger (p. 109). But the fact remains that sun-sacrifice is a pervasive trope in colonial-racist writing.

7. ..."*Tintin... Apocalypto*"

See the Tintin title "Prisoners of the Sun." Our adoration for Tintin and his friends aside, we must also recognize the colonial-era prejudices that played out in many titles in the series (the worst was Tintin in the Congo).

The human sacrifice trope was also the center of the 2006 film Apocalypto, a sort of backlash statement against white liberal guilt from Mel Gibson, apparently. See the following for more on the movie's myths and fantasies:

Zachary X. Hruby (December 11 2006). Apocalypto Does Disservice to its Subjects. *The San Francisco Chronicle*.

Lest we believe these examples only come from pop culture and are therefore inconsequential, we need look no further than the otherwise scientific Stephen Pinker's data-thumping ode to the non-violence seeking Western civilization, *The Better Angels of Our Nature*. We find very little questioning of these and other Indiana Jones- style colonial myths about *thuggees* and such in his book as well:

Stephen Pinker (2011). *The Better Angels of Our Nature: Why Violence has Declined*. New York: Penguin.

8. *"monsoon ... whimsical and violent gods"*
Doniger, *The Hindus*, p. 62.

9. *"They did not believe... plant-based diet."*
Tristram Stuart (2006). *The Bloodless Revolution: Radical Vegetarians and the Discovery of India*. New York: Harper.

10. *"ice-age mental factory"*
Survivalism is one of the most pervasive and invisible ideologies in modernity. I recall a classroom conversation in India in the 1970s, when our substitute teacher got called in to settle an argument between two nine year olds on a "veg and non-veg" question. The teacher's response was: 'what if you are in a plane crash and end up on an island? There you will have to eat what you must to survive, no?' It seemed smart and practical then. But now, it seems different. That was the cultural aftermath of Nehru's India; modern, open-minded; no doubt, but too open to the possibility perhaps of a class full of children most of whom have never even been on a plane crashing, surviving, and then ending up on an island where there are mysteriously no fruits but presumably, 'game'.

11. *"belief that violence and nature..."*
Foer makes an important distinction between violence and cruelty. The latter, he says, is based on knowing whether or not an action is cruel, and then choosing to ignore its consequences. Nature might be violent, but to be systematically cruel, it appears, is a largely human failure.

Jonathan Safran Foer (2009). *Eating Animals*. New York: Little Brown.

12. *"They are not living bloodshed as a way of life, thought, and culture."*
Again, Parekh's summary of Gandhi's critique of violence is a fantastic summary. Also see the movie *Naqoyqatsi*, a way of life based on killing, for a sense of an artistic representation of such a recognition.

13. *"how pervasive and widespread the naturalization of violence is today. It is no longer one of many elements in the media, but almost the entirety of the media environment itself."*

As George Gerbner, one of the pioneering figures in media violence research puts it, "we are awash in a tide of violent representations such as the world has never seen before". And this, presumably, was long before either *Game of Thrones* in America, or crime news programs in India. The main finding of Gerbner's research, the Mean World Syndrome, tells us that heavy TV viewing is associated among viewers with a perception of the real world as being more dangerous than it really is. Media violence may not cause real life acts of violence, but it has been demonstrated to have a bearing on how we think, and what we assume is normal or natural.

Michael Morgan (2002). *Against the Mainstream: The Selected Works of George Gerbner*. New York: Peter Lang.

14. *"Hindu is 'Himsa' and 'duramu'"*
A saying of Sri Sathya Sai Baba. I state this here as an example of how much importance the ideal of ahimsa continues to be accorded by important religious figures in India.

15. *"The Englishman..."*
A famous doggerel from the time of Gandhi's early life, discussed in:

Arvind Sharma (2013). *Gandhi: A Spiritual Biography*. New Haven: Yale.

It is also instructive that Gandhi's first public writings were in the context of his encounter with European vegetarianism while in London. See:

Ramachandra Guha (October 5, 2013) Mahatma Gandhi: Experiments with Eating. *LiveMint*.

16. *"During colonialism, diet, Darwin, and racism all came together conveniently in the colonizer's fantasy."*
Jeremy Rifkin refers to the writings of George Beard, an influential 19th century racial theorist who argued that "the superior races of human beings were naturally disposed to eat higher up on the world's food chain" (247). He also quotes Beard: "the rice-eating Hindu and Chinese and the potato-eating Irish peasant are kept in subjection by the well fed English." Wendy Doniger's endnote reference to vegetarianism in India should also be seen closely in reference to the persistence of dietary mythology from the colonial era: she notes that sixty per cent of people in Rajasthan and Haryana — *where seafood is not available* — are vegetarian, and that in Gandhi's Gujarat, *which is predominantly landlocked* (sic.) forty-five per cent of the people are vegetarian (p. 705). It is apparently more convenient

to attribute vegetarianism to geography rather than acknowledge that there is a powerful ethical tradition against animal-killing in Indian life and thought! Even if other factors play a role today in what people eat and don't eat (conspicuous consumption, status, and poverty too, no denying it), we can't deny that Indian ethical vegetarianism, colonial and postcolonial dietary normativity, and casteism in Indian vegetarianism, all need to be understood accurately and with due attention to each of them.

Jeremy Rifkin (1993). *Beyond Beef: The Rise and Fall of the Cattle Complex*. New York: Plume.

17. *"This, too, is a real example".*
The Eat-a-bug Cookbook, an exemplary artifact of hunter-gatherer instinct, was discovered at the gift shop of the otherwise wonderful Lawrence Berkeley Hall of Science, Berkeley, California.

Chapter 5. The Myth of a Hindu View of History ...

1. *"pigs in Animal Farm" "...sort of polytheism in the Vedas"*
Doniger, *The Hindus*, p. 129

2. *"...epics ... tall tales told by charioteers"*
Doniger, *The Hindus*, p. 218

3. *"...'tension' between Rama, Sita and Lakshmana"*
Doniger, *The Hindus*, p. 237

4. *"Valmiki ... interruption of the crane's sexual act"*
Doniger, *The Hindus*, p. 243

5. *"If you say it's about sex or violence, it's suddenly 'reality'...."*
The legal scholar Jeffrey Rosen offers an insightful explanation about the equation of sexuality with truth, so to speak, in late modern societies. Following Giddens on the evacuation of trust in modernity, Rosen suggests that sexual identity, or privacy, more broadly, ends up becoming a way of gauging "who someone really is" in a world of strangers. This is not to say sexuality is not important, especially when it comes to rights and empowerment, but its sophomoric application in religious studies needs to be seen as one more mythology of our times with very little bearing on what Hinduism means.

Jeffrey Rosen (2004). *The Naked Crowd: Reclaiming Security and Freedom in an Anxious Age*. New York: Random House.

6. *"Ramayana is a work of fiction"*
Doniger, *The Hindus*, p. 662

7 *"... an old racist colonial myth about the dynamics between white women and people of colour."*
Frantz Fanon (1967). *White Skin, Black Masks*. New York: Grove.

8 *"... gods as being just like us, seeking things like marriage, adultery and flattery"*
Doniger, *The Hindus*, p. 130

9. *"Like the Lingam, another long story, translation without respect for truth is a form of terrorism"*
One of Wendy Doniger's persistent claims is on the alleged "phallic" meaning of the Shiva Lingam; often entirely at the expense of acknowledging the existence of other meanings. Diana Eck, in her more realistic study of Hinduism's sacred geography, writes that the Lingam represents an "epiphany" of such cosmic proportions that it could hardly be reduced to its one interpretation as anatomy. The peculiar body and gaze equation between Hinduism and Western observers is perhaps something that scholars could address more carefully in the future. It is funny, sometimes, to see even affectionate observers of India like the travelogue narrator Michael Wood talk about Nataraja's "abs" in the PBS series *The Story of India*, rather than the usual things we notice about sacred images like the smile or the eyes.

Diane Eck (2012). *India: A Sacred Geography*. New York: Harmony.

10. *"Partition ...Vedic culture of revering violence"*
Doniger, *The Hindus*, p. 627.

11. *"...diet better suited for surviving global warming rather than the last ice age"*
The debate on food politics in India tends, for understandable reasons, to head in the opposite direction from what progressive food choices might seem like in Western societies. In India, our debate still seems to react very touchily to this question since it is unfortunately tied up with issues of caste and exclusion. We should recognize that diet was used in caste discrimination, but strive towards expressing the

ethical and environmental concerns around diet on their own terms too. Books like *Fast Food Nation, The Sexual Politics of Meat, Eating Animals, Meatonomics*, and others have raised a tremendous degree of conscientious reflection around the world on the ecological and ethical issues involved with an industrial meat-heavy diet. Another billion people eating McBurgers is probably not a very sustainable way to fight the casteism that vegetarianism came with in the past. America has given its poor the empty promise of seemingly inexpensive food in the form of the burger; but its cost is enormous. It ruins the health of the poor, and comes at enormous social and environmental cost to the planet in terms of deforestation (for grazing land), water and grain use, and global warming (the most energy intensive and expensive food to create is sold as the cheapest one, and there is obviously a hidden cost somewhere).

Carol Adams (2004). *The Pornography of Meat*. Bloomsbury Academic.

Eric Schlosser (2002) *Fast Food Nation: The Dark Side of the All American Meal*. New York: Harper Perennial.

Jonathan Safran Foer (2009). *Eating Animals*. New York: Little, Brown & Co.

David Simons (2013). *Meatonomics*. California: Conari Press.

Vaclav Smil (2012). *Should We Eat Meat?: Evolution and Consequences of Modern Carnivory*. Chichester, UK : Wiley-Blackwell.

T. Colin Campbell & Thomas Campbell (2005). *The China Study*. Dallas: BenBella Books.

12. *"We are fed up of hearing Ganesha is a symbol of our fears of mutilation."*
Nussbaum appears to believe that the controversy over Paul Courtright's book on Ganesha was caused by his comparison of Ganesha's trunk to a *limp* penis – as if the issue was Hindu machismo rather than a brazen disregard for sensibility. A simple piece of information for scholars here – devout Hindus think of Shiva as they would their father, and Ganesha and Krishna as they would their own children. Sexualizing child-gods is as offensive therefore as sexualizing children in one's writing.

13. *"… world that kills elephants"*
Elephant executions were truly among the most appalling spectacles in the last days of an earlier era of pubic animal trials. Thomas Edison not only provided the know-how, but also filmed one such event in a documentary

entitled "Electrocuting the Elephant." I am drawing particular attention to issues of animal abuse and Hinduism distortion here because both issues, in my view, are closely interconnected. We will understand Hinduism a lot better if we recognize how much the modern world has warped our understanding of the living world by objectifying it. As Hribal writes in his book about captured animals' struggles to escape, these animals "have a conception of freedom and a desire for it. They have agency." While modern India may be guilty too of animal abuse, exploitation and violence, it is my belief *that Hindu thought* still contains far more space for recognizing animal agency than modern anthropocentrism; and when we respect that space, we will also be able to refute Hinduphobia more strongly for what it is.

Jason Hribal (2010). *Fear of the Animal Planet: The Hidden History of Animal Resistance*. California: CounterPunch and AK Press.

PART 2. SANATHANA

Chapter 1. Prelude

1. *"Aspiration, and hope, both belong to the people."*
The writings of Amish Tripathi, Anand Neelakantan, Devdutt Pattanaik, and others mark, in my view, nothing less than a civilizational surge of interest in questions about who we are, and why we think and act the way we do.

2. *"Civilization lurks in unknown places, in the smallest of things and gestures."*
I think of two images, one fictional, and the other real, but both about dignity in the face of poverty and deprivation. The first is a scene from Jerry Pinto's wonderful novel *Em and the Big Hoom*, when the protagonist is shocked by a poor hungry man on the road who refuses to accept non-vegetarian food. Though the term "beggars can't be choosers" might come to mind, we must recognize that our tendency to dismiss such a move would be presumptuous and not appreciative enough of the ethical commitment people make about not taking life, even among the poor. The second example is an image from the 1999 American TV news special *Is America Number 1?* The host John Stossel wanders among beggars and homeless people in India. But what the camera voyeurizes

as third world spectacle, is somehow also belied by contradictions of a sort Stossel probably does not see; a poor mother living on the edge of a construction site is cleaning her child's bottom, with water, using her left hand. Without any romanticism one can still recognize that poverty too does not erase a human being's code of meaning and value over hygiene and body. On the other hand, the five star hotel where the host most likely stayed perhaps catered to civilization more by sending reams of paper into the drain each day.

Chapter 2. Tvameva, You Alone (Veda and Upanishad)

1. *"the colonization of India and the Americas to the Native American displacement, has been connected to the rise of the beef industry"*
Jeremy Rifkin discusses this in *Beyond Beef*. Rifkin shows us how central cattle have been to the history of the world, and perhaps future scholarship could create for us a better account of how central the cow has been to Hindu thought and history.

Jeremy Rifkin (1990). *Beyond Beef: The Rise and Fall of the Cattle Complex*. New York: Plume.

Also see:

Florian Werner (2011). *Cow: A Bovine Biography*. Vancouver: Greystone.

2. *"We are, one might say, 'spiritual anarchists.'*
Naturally, this upsets people like Hitler! I borrow the phrase from this delightful Indian elections parody of *Inglorious Basterds*:

http://www.youtube.com/watch?v=ibW9iDMcrPs

3. *"We speak also of 330 million gods."*
This figure has been widely mentioned to make all sorts of points, from Hinduism's pluralism to its alleged superstitions. Sri Sathya Sai Baba's parable is instructive: when the phrase was coined, he says, there were 330 million people living in the world, and it only means everyone is sacred! Devdutt Pattanaik makes a useful suggestion that the figure represents the diversity of forms through which we appreciate the divine, rather than a literal representation.

Devdutt Pattanaik (2006). *Myth=Mithya: A Handbook of Hindu Mythology*. New Delhi: Penguin.

Chapter 3. Cousins and Friends

1. *"Our stories about Krishna and Rama…"*

See Devdutt Pattanaik's commentary on the need to cultivate Indian ways of looking at Indian mythology; we are moving generationally, from living in "mythology" as stories about the gods, with their own unspoken epistemologies, to a more modern, anthropocentric worldview of trying to see them as either superheroes or as ancient conquerors. In this chapter, I try to point out what makes our perennial classics so perennial; they speak to the human condition in ways even we don't always realize.

Devdutt Pattanaik (June 29, 2014). How We Read Mythology. *Mid-Day*.

2. *"Our experience of God is as good as our depictions of it."*

See Diana Eck's book *Darsan* for a well-informed discussion of "representation" in Hindu life and philosophy. In a way, we do not distinguish between "form" and "content" when it comes to sacred representations. The amount of reverence we offer to depictions of our gods and goddesses is an indication of how seriously our culture took the power of language and art, and despite the challenges of media proliferation today that renders representation into banality, we must not lose sight of it.

Diana Eck (1998). *Darsan: Seeing the Divine Image in India*. New York: Columbia.

3. *"He doles out food…."*

Comment made by His Holiness the Mathadhipathi at the Udupi Krishna temple, Guru Purnima, 2008.

4 *"Sita is a symbol of submissiveness as Rama is a symbol of patriarchy"*
See:

Malashri Lal & Namita Gokhale (2010). *In Search of Sita: Revisiting Mythology*. New Delhi: Penguin.

5. *"Rama, in the Mahatma's voice."*

The discussion of Gandhi's devotion for Rama as historical figure and as formless god is useful. See Parekh, *Gandhi: A Very Short Introduction* and also Sharma, *Gandhi: A Spiritual Biography*.

6. *"…that monkey, that Hanuman"*
A reference to a memorable line from William Buck's masterful, poetic and beautiful *Ramayana*: "who is this monkey, this Hanuman? Rama has let him loose in the world. He knows Rama and Rama knows him" (427).

William Buck (1976). *Ramayana*. Berkeley: University of California.

7. *"We rule ourselves, for the ones we want to rule ourselves for."*
My take on Mahatma Gandhi's idea of *swaraj* as not merely freedom from foreign rule, but more as the striving for freedom from any force that denies us sovereignty over our own selves; greed, possessiveness, resentfulness, and so on.

M.K. Gandhi (2009/1909). *Hind Swaraj and Other Writings* (Anthony Parel, ed.). Cambridge: Cambridge University Press.

8. *"It is not until one's relationship with the other is right."*
I often think of this as a truly brilliant "meaning of everything" quote; from Chaturvedi Badrinath's insightful discussion of what the *Mahabharatha* says, about everything from agency and determination to governance and force.

Chaturvedi Badrinath (2006). *The Mahabharatha: An Inquiry in the Human Condition*. Hyderabad: Orient Longman.

Chapter 4. The Greatest Love

1. *"As Yudhisthira tells the Yaksha of the Lake, what is inevitable is not death, as we often think, but happiness. "*
An elegantly stated stunner of a line from Peter Brook's *Mahabharatha*.

2 *"In any case, it is not always natural for human beings to feel remorseless about killing."*

Lt. Colonel Dave Grossman (1995). *On Killing: The Psychological Cost of Learning to Kill in War and Society*. New York: Hachette.

3. *"… separation of life into human and animal."*
Once again, this remains one of the relatively unexamined areas of prejudice in academics, though this hierarchy is one of the definitive features of modernity. In India, a premodern sensibility still remains, even if it is somewhat mixed up and unclearly articulated in the public debate.

It is unfortunate that sensibilities around animals are often dismissed by Hinduphobes as superstition and "primitive animal worship." Interestingly, for a project that lists "animals" as one of the "alternative" voices it seeks to recuperate, Doniger's *The Hindus* is obdurately anthropocentric in its treatment of animals — they are treated mostly as metaphors for human groups and actions, and seldom as living, sentient beings on their terms. Malhotra and Neelakandan also point out that the insistence on reading animals in Hinduism as metaphors for subaltern groups is a pervasive feature of the argument made by proselytization movements in India. While legitimate subaltern grievances ought not to be dismissed, it is also important to not suppress the fact that animal depictions in Hindu thought are probably more about the recognition of animal subjectivity and agency than anything else. Hindu thought is an important resource for the emerging field of animal studies, and conversely, Hindu history cannot be understood accurately without respecting the very different place that animals had in premodern life and thought. Virtually every god and goddess is associated with an animal, as we know, and what that means is an essential question for future scholarship.

For a very useful discussion of animals in Indian thought see:

Nanditha Krishna (2010). *Sacred Animals of India*. New Delhi: Penguin.

For a broader historical discussion of the human/animal divide in modernity, see:

Joanna Bourke (2011). *What it means to be human*. Berkeley: Counterpoint.

Paul Waldau. (2013). *Animal Studies: An Introduction*. Oxford: OUP.

For a popular scientific account of animal "voice" in nature and reality see:

Tim Friend (2004). *Animal Talk: Breaking the Codes of Animal Language*. New York: Free Press.

It is also worth recalling Jason Hribal's reference to an African saying here: "Until the lion has his historian, the hunter will always be the hero."

4. *"... great religious myths have been interpreted as metaphors for the horror of killing animals for food..."*
Tristram Stuart writes that "Europe's encounter with Indian vegetarianism had a *massive impact* well beyond the radical fringe" in the 17th and 18th

centuries, around the same time as the scientific revolution. Perhaps the reexamination of religious sanction for the domination of humans over animals that began at that time could be continued once again by historians and theologians in the future. Also see:

Ryn Berry (1998). *Food for the Gods: Vegetarianism and the World's Religions*. New York: Pythagorean Publisher.

5. "... Thus cogitated Descartes"

Tristram Stuart tells the story of some of Descartes' enthusiastic followers who beat up dogs in the street in order to make a "scientific" point to shocked bystanders that the cries of the poor dogs were no different from the sounds of a machine or inanimate object being struck. They laughed at people who were pained, dismissing their concern for the animal as unscientific. Pinker also refers to this story, not unsympathetically to animals, in *The Better Angels of Our Nature* as well. Unfortunately, in his eagerness perhaps to attribute to Western civilization the credit for discovering animal rights, he dismisses Hindu vegetarianism as mere superstition about reincarnation—a common Western myth that holds that Hindus who are vegetarian are that way out of fear of ingesting a reincarnated ancestor, rather than out of simple ethical choice.

6. "things we pretend don't matter about animals..."

Jonathan Safran Foer's observation that a culture that ignores animal suffering is likely to also ignore human suffering is important to bear in mind when confronted by accusations that concern for animal suffering is somehow an elite issue and neglects human suffering. Whether it is the objectification of women's bodies as "meat" and the sexualization of meat in meat product ads, as Carol Adams shows, or in the ruthless scientism that reached its peak in the Nazi camps (Florian Werner notes that 'animal husbandry' techniques were deployed scrupulously in the holocaust), we cannot dismiss the fact that there do exist similarities between the kinds of cruelty we show to humans to animals alike. We live in a culture of systemic denial of the pain of other living creatures; resensitizing us to the pain of humans too perhaps becomes that much more challenging as a result.

7. "Dasavatar..."

Doniger claims the avatars of *Vishnu* got classified in the evolutionary direction only since the 1880s. The fact that Jayadeva, Madhva, Ramanuja, Raghavendra, and many other saints and scholars celebrated the *Dasavatar* in poetry for far longer though suggests that the idea of recognizing the sacred in specific non-human forms is much older than more recent attempts to see (or deny) evolution in them. For a serious scholarly study of Hindu philosophy, modern science, and nature, see Jonathan Edelman's new book:

Jonathan Edelman (2013). *Hindu Theology and Biology*. New York: Oxford.

8. "…*evolution was somehow figured out before Darwin by an Arab scientist.*"
I state this not as a denial of the contributions of Arab science to the West and to world knowledge but as a reminder that the project of decentering Eurocentric historiography has to go even further. See, for example:

Jim Al Khalili (January 29, 2008). It's Time to Herald the Arabic Science that Prefigured Newton and Darwin. *The Guardian*.

Chapter 5. Teacher

1. *"Shankara, Ramanuja, Madhva."*
Strangely but not unsurprisingly, Doniger's treatment of these three important philosophers is distorted and dismissive, aimed perhaps at bolstering the Hinduphobic denial of Hinduism's scholarly lineages and indeed, existential validity. Arvind Sharma's work, among others, is more useful for serious students.

Arvind Sharma (1986). *The Hindu Gita*. London: Duckworth.

2. *"Sai."*
For reasoned and non-mystifying accounts of the Sai Baba phenomenon see:

Arnold Schulman (1971). *Baba*. New York: Viking.

Bill Aitken (2004). *Sri Sathya Sai Baba: A Life*. New Delhi: Viking.

Smriti Srinivas (2008). *In the Presence of Sai Baba: Body, City and Memory in a Global Movement*. Hyderabad: Orient Longman.

Vamsee Juluri (forthcoming). *The Guru Within*. Chennai: Westland.

3. *"… Krishna lives in our hearts and in our lives in ways that cannot be explained away."*
Mahatma Gandhi's insight from his commentary on the *Gita* is useful for us as we confront our highly polarized debates today on whether Krishna belongs to "history" or "mythology." He writes: "Krishna of the Gita is perfection

and right knowledge personified; but the picture is imaginary. That does not mean Krishna, the adored of his people, never lived. But perfection is imagined". The "power" of Krishna, in other words, has everything to do with our sensibilities, with how we perceive him in our hearts, minds, and culture. As a student of popular culture, I feel pained by depictions that tend to lose sight of ethical and aesthetic balance in depicting sacred stories. I do not know if there are "true" or "false" interpretations, but I do know some representations *feel* more sacred than others.

Mahatma Gandhi (2002/1931). *Bhagavad Gita: The Song of God*. Kent: Axiom.

4. *"Otherwise, we might be blaming Krishna for our own faults and failings."*
Alluding here to a saying of Mahatma Gandhi's that whatever good we do is because of god and whatever bad we do is probably our own fault! I believe it is a good way for cultivating unselfishness; we learn gratitude and appreciation for whatever is good about our place in this earth, and we assume responsibility for changing whatever is not.

5 *"… end of all our striving…"*
Moksha is best understood, according to Badrinath, not as some metaphysical or religious idea, but as a secular, and one might say, universal ideal. It is not "escape from" as we often conceive it, but merely "freedom into." Moksha, he suggests, is simply "an invitation to the newness of everything".

6. *"Five senses … one Krishna"*
Paramahamsa Yogananda (2007). *The Yoga of the Bhagavad Gita*. Los Angeles: Self Realization Fellowship.

7. *"… in today's world of work and life"*
For an insightful study of what the Gita means in today's life without being reduced to a mere coping philosophy, see Gurcharan Das's *The Difficulty of Being Good*, a vivid account of ethics as a lived, historical idea in contemporary India.

Gurcharan Das (2009). *The Difficulty of Being Good: On the Subtle Art of Dharma*. New York: Oxford.

8. *"… technicism… a blind faith in technique…"*
Ashis Nandy, From Outside the Imperium; Bhikhu Parekh on means and ends in *Gandhi: A Very Short Introduction*.

9. *"Satyameva Jayate still stands, but in a perverted way...."*
Thanks to Adithya Yaga for this story. For more thoughts on the cultural resonance of the phrase in India (and the TV show) see:

Vamsee Juluri (2012). Satyamev Jayate: Truth is God in India's New TV Show. *The Huffington Post.*

10. *"You quote lines about Shiva..."*
See Oppenheimer's much quoted line from the Gita, and also the "Shiva, God of Death" epiphany in the 2007 movie *Michael Clayton*. There is perhaps a tendency to see Hinduism with a greater emphasis on destructiveness and fatalism from Western viewpoints than in Hindu everyday life. It may also be helpful if we paid attention to nuances, like thinking of Shiva as the god of "dissolution," rather than "destruction" ourselves!

11. *"It is every crime against decency, dignity, life, and truth that is spread out before you."*
It may be worth recalling "Gandhi's Talisman" here: "Recall the face of the poorest and weakest you have seen... ask yourself if the step you contemplate will be of any use to him." I am grateful to Prof. Sivakumar for reminding me of this important idea during his visit to my Gandhi in the Media class. In my view, these words of the Mahatma are indeed the equivalent of *Krishna*'s admonition to *Arjuna* for our own time and place in history. It is an apt antidote for the inevitable selfishness, narcissism, and distraction from reality that a cultural environment defined by consumerism creates.

12. *"Mother Earth. Brother Labour."*
If there is one key philosophical idea I had to mention as essential to Hindu sensibilities, it is the notion of *karma*, of cause and effect, debt and obligation. We need not see this in mystical terms alone, but in rational, material forms as well. In premodern societies, our debts were obvious; most of us lived in villages, and we knew where everything came from. Exploitation was real, but transparent. In today's highly mediated global economy, most of the things we consume, the food that makes our bodies, the clothes we wear, the energy we consume, all of these come from the labor of people we cannot see. Our debt to nature and labor, our "*karma* footprint," so to speak, is enormous; even if we justify our consumption to ourselves as reward for our own hard work and enterprise. So for Hindu

reasons, if not for the sake of Marxist ideologies, it is useful for us to recognize, always, the conditions that create us, sustain us, and give us an obligation to act in certain ways, which we might choose to call *dharmic* ways, according to our best interpretation of both *sanathana* and *desa-kala*. Devdutt Pattanaik's summary of actions that earn merit and debt in his *Myth=Mithya* is useful, and so is Parekh's discussion of Gandhi's idea that we are all "born debtors" in his *Gandhi: A Very Short Introduction*. Also watch the documentary "The Story of Stuff" (www.storyofstuff.org). All of this might make you think of "Mother Nature, Brother Labour," more often, and in more unexpected ways too.

Conclusion: Jagat Guru

1. *"Jagat Guru"*
This is a reference to a phrase from Prime Minister Narendra Modi's May 17, 2014 speech in Varanasi. The significance of this moment, in my view, was not in its mere symbolism, but in the precise choice of words uttered by him at this time when the world was indeed watching. The suggestion he made was not just that India had something to teach the world, which would have been a mere slogan, but that India had *something to learn* too, even if from itself. My optimism about the present moment comes in large part from things like this, things I view as a very Indian kind of intelligence; adventurous and respectful, progressive and conservative, practical, and still, somehow ethical.

2. *"...colonialism's one-eyed vision..."*
Thomas Merton (1964). Introduction: Gandhi and the One-Eyed Giant. From *Gandhi on Non-Violence*. New York: New Directions.

3 *"...jellyfish..."*
Carl Engelking (April 2014). Eco-friendly diapers made from jellyfish. *Discover*.

ACKNOWLEDGMENTS

I gratefully acknowledge C. Sriram's careful critique and suggestions. I am also thankful to Vijay Das for a spot-check on the Hampi Lakshmi-Narasimha, and to my extended family for their wonderful hospitality in Hampi some years ago.

My thanks also to Chetan Sandhir for sharing his splendid photograph for the cover, to Poosapati Parameshwar Raju for his exquisite calligraphy, to Lakshmi Prabhala and Mark Ulyseas for the photos of sculptures.

I thank Sadhana Ramchander and the Blue Pencil Infodesign team, for the design and typesetting of this book.

My thanks to Gautam Padmanabhan, Karthik Venkatesh and everyone at Westland Publishing for rising to the moment with prompt support for this project.

Finally, my thanks to L and V, who have filled the absence of a world that vanished suddenly and violently from me with love, and more love, until suddenly, it all seems clear again; this is fullness, and whatever anyone thinks they take out of it, still, only fullness remains.